JOHN GIRVAN
For Christ and His Church

JOHN W. LOCKINGTON

AMBASSADOR INTERNATIONAL
Greenville, South Carolina • Belfast, Northern Ireland

JOHN GIRVAN: FOR CHRIST AND HIS CHURCH

ISBN 1   84030 162 7

Ambassador Publications
a division of
Ambassador Productions Ltd.
Providence House
Ardenlee Street,
Belfast,
BT6 8QJ
Northern Ireland
www.ambassador-productions.com

Emerald House
427 Wade Hampton Blvd.
Greenville
SC 29609, USA
www.emeraldhouse.com

CONTENTS

FOREWORD

Dr John Lockington has earned the gratitude of very many by writing this account of the life and ministry of the late Dr John Girvan.

The book is first and foremost a loving tribute to a thoroughgoing Christian, a man of prayer, a devoted minister, an effective evangelist and a genuine friend. Many who have been blessed and helped through Dr Girvan will be very glad to have in their hands this expression of appreciation which they have felt but have not had opportunity to show.

But under God it will have a much wider influence. For those who are aware of a call to Christian service there will be encouragement to take positive steps to prepare themselves for work at home or overseas; for those who are in the regular ministry there will be the challenge to do the work of an evangelist, and for those who are half-hearted believers there will be repeated prompting to wholly follow the Lord.

And it may be that in the Divine providence some who were not far from the Kingdom in one of Dr Girvan's ministries

or missions may hear the call again as they read this book and
be altogether persuaded to become Christians.

Very Rev Dr W M Craig

AUTHOR'S ACKNOWLEDGEMENTS

When it was first suggested that something be placed on record of the life and ministry of John Girvan five men met to consider the possibility. Very Rev Dr William M Craig, Rev Dr Jackson C Buick, Rev Dr Brian Moore and Mr Victor Malcolmson entrusted the honour and responsibility to me to produce this volume but their help with research and their prayers, fellowship and support have been a continual encouragement.

I am grateful that Dr W M Craig, a life long friend of John's, agreed to write the Foreword. The deep love of both men for each other and their Lord and the Church they served has been an inspiration to so many.

This book would not have appeared at all without the agreement of Mary and I want to express profound thanks to her for the information and insights she provided. John's sisters, Belle and Jean also made valuable contributions.

My sincere thanks to Mrs Moira Craig, Senior Librarian, Central Library, Londonderry, to Mr Alan McMillan, Assistant Secretary and Librarian of the Presbyterian Historical Society, to

Mr George Ferguson, the Executive Secretary of the Belfast City Mission, to Rev Dudley L Cooney, Archivist of Irish Christian Endeavour, and to the TBF and the KL Thompson Trust.

I wish to thank the Ministers and Kirk Sessions of Carlisle Road, Immanuel and Hill Street Presbyterian Churches for making congregational records available and for their permission to use whatever might prove beneficial in thanksgiving for their late pastor and friend.

I have appreciated assistance from those individuals whose names are mentioned in the text as well as the co-operation of many others who have willingly shared their experiences and have supplied information.

A number of people have provided the photographs and thanks is due for their permission to reproduce them.

I wish to thank my wife Norma for her assistance, encouragement and patience.

Every effort has been made to check facts but if there are any inaccuracies please accept my apologies.

John W Lockington

1

EARLY DAYS

In 1917 the First World War was in its fourth year. Germany launched a campaign of unrestricted submarine warfare and the United States of America entered the war. London was bombed for the first time and fierce fighting took place at Arras and Ypres. British troops captured Baghdad. Alexander Kerensky formed a provisional government in Russia when Tsar Nicholas II abdicated. One year after the rebellion in Dublin, Prime Minister Lloyd George called an Irish Convention attended by Unionist and Nationalist delegates, which proved unsuccessful. Harland and Wolff invested £1 million to build a forty-one acre yard on the east side of the Musgrave Channel in Belfast.

People could buy a man's shirt for five shillings and six pence (28p) and ladies stockings for one shilling and sixpence (8p). A suit cost fifty shillings (£2.50p) and a new top of the range bicycle cost £19. Butter was two shillings per pound (10p) and soap three pence (1p). A 'kitchen house' off the Crumlin

Road, Belfast could be purchased for £175 and a double bed could be provided for fifty five shillings (£2.75p).

At Killinchy, Co Down on 6th August that year the third of the the six children of James and Jane Girvan was born and given the name of John. James was a labourer who later worked on the construction of the Parliament Buildings at Stormont. A native of Killinchy, he had married Jane McVeigh from Lisbarnett on 16th May 1913 in Killinchy Presbyterian Church. They set up home first in Killinchy and eventually came to live at Kilmood. Along with John, his older sister, Mary, and his younger sisters, Jean and Belle, were the only children to survive infancy.

John grew up in a home where, like many rural cottages at that time, there were none of the modern conveniences of 21st century life. Even as a young boy he was extraordinarily helpful to his mother, who was disabled for some 30 years, carrying in the coal and wood for the fire and fetching water from a nearby well. On one such occasion John decided to make life a bit easier for himself. Instead of filling the large bucket by using the small bucket several times, he tried to fill the large bucket at one go. When he attempted to lift the large bucket he overbalanced and fell into the well. Providentially, a neighbour, Mr. Osborne, was working in a nearby field and heard him and quickly came to his rescue.

Jeannie Lowry (now Peake) was in John's class in Lisbarnett Public Elementary School and recalls that even then John showed musical ability and forthrightness. He was one of the few pupils who could read the music the schoolmaster put on the board for the singing lesson. But he was not reticent about asking " Can we not sing what we want? " and sometimes the master relented and allowed the pupils to choose.

Like many children, any diversion from school was welcome. From time to time the County Down Hunt used the lane alongside the school. The sound of the hounds excited the children, including John, who followed them, only to be 'slapped' by the master when they arrived late for the roll call.

He is remembered by his contemporaries as someone who was full of vigour. He himself admitted "I was not a particularly good boy". That was an opinion shared by the schoolmaster at Lisbarnett School, who remarked about him and his friends "You are the worst set of boys I ever taught!" However the school mistress had a different opinion. "Girvan" she said to him "if you put that energy to better use, you might make something worthwhile of yourself". Little did she know that such energy surrendered to God was to be used to have a tremendous impact for the gospel.

From an early age John loved riding his bicycle. There was nothing he enjoyed more than travelling along the roads all around the district and exploring the countryside with his best friend, Harry Clements. But he was well known for his recklessness.

Once he was told to go to the Post Office to collect a letter from America. Just then a bus stopped near the house. In order to get there quickly John tried to catch hold of the bus and run behind it. For some reason his clothing was caught and he was dragged along the road for about 150 yards until someone managed to get the bus stopped. His knees were badly cut and had to be bathed three times a day in salt water and methylated spirit. He bore those scars the rest of his life, but they didn't keep him off his bike!

His parents were members of St Mary's Church of Ireland at Kilmood, where John was baptized and confirmed and where he sang in the Church Choir as well as working the bellows for the organ. No organization for boys existed in Kilmood Church. So, when a Boys' Brigade Company was formed on 11th December 1930 in Ballygowan Presbyterian Church, about one and a half miles away, John became a founder member. There were some 48 boys with seven officers, including Jacob Haire as

Captain and Rev Dr William McLernon as Chaplain. For John it was the beginning of a life-long commitment to the organization. He revelled in the drill, Physical Education, the discipline and football, rising through the ranks to that of staff sergeant.

John remarked "My mother was a marvellous woman. Although she did not suffer so much pain she experienced much frustration. Still there was no complaint and no rebellion against God". She had a significant influence on all her children. Many years later John spoke of her with reference to family worship. "I remember my mother gathering her little family around her, particularly on Sunday evenings, and singing hymns and praying. I believe it did something to me and for me."

She prayed earnestly for her children and encouraged others to do so too.

In 1932 Mr. James Gibson of Dundonald came to conduct a Mission in a tent in a field in Lisbarnett, and with the encouragement of his mother and at the invitation of a Boys' Brigade friend, Harry Scott, John attended the meetings. On Friday 26th May he waited behind to speak to the missioner. He explained that he was seeking the Saviour. For a time he could not understand and then Mr. Gibson read to him Isaiah 53:5 'He was wounded for our transgressions, he was bruised for our iniquities; the chastisement of our peace was upon him and with his stripes we are healed'. He told John to read it for himself putting his own name where the words 'our' and 'we' were. John read 'He was wounded for John Girvan's transgressions, he was bruised for John Girvan's iniquities; the chastisement of John Girvan's peace was upon him and with his stripes John Girvan is healed.' The light of the truth of the substitutionary death of Jesus Christ dawned on him and he immediately received Him as his Saviour. It was a decisive point in John's life from which he never looked back.

He later would say about that time in his life "My greatest desire as a young believer was that I might not fail God. I can remember that I exploited every means to that end. I made friends of God's people, attended meetings, regardless of age group, witnessed for the Lord as well as I could, prayed and read my Bible. I began reading at Genesis and went right through to Revelation. I did that eleven times. All that required discipline. I did not receive any instruction as to how to read the Bible, I simply got on with it".

Ballygowan Flute Band had started in 1876 in the village and up to the present day has been one of the most prestigious flute bands in Ireland. John's interest in and enthusiasm for music had led him as a teenager to join the band. In the short time he was a member he learned to play the flute, an ability he never lost. But there were other things that took up more and more of his time and attention.

He continued at Lisbarnett Public Elementary School until he was 16. This was in the early 1930's when work was scarce and in fact at that time his father was unemployed. John was fortunate when he obtained work in the coach building business of Robert Harkness & Sons in Dover Street off the Shankill Road in Belfast. William Clements ran a bus service in East Belfast and had a summer cottage near Drumreagh. John was friendly with William's children and their father mentioned John's name to the owners of the firm of Harkness who built his buses. They were later to enquire of him that, if he knew of any other young men of the quality of John Girvan, he could be assured that they would gladly take them on as apprentices.

From the beginning of his Christian life John was determined to take his stand for the Lord in his work place and he did so with courage and sensitivity. Typically he was burdened for those men with whom he worked but wondered how he could witness to them. He decided to start by whistling hymns which inevitably had the effect of opening up conversations. But something which made a deep impression on them was his practical interest in the homes and families of the men with whom he worked.

Employment in Belfast involved riding his bicycle four miles to Comber station in all weathers followed by a train journey to the Queen's Quay Station in Belfast and then a tram journey across the city to work. For John it meant rising at 5:45 am, making his breakfast and having his quiet time with the Lord in prayer and Bible study before he left home. His homeward journey took some time but, however late or tired he was, he ensured that he was present at whatever meeting took place that evening. While serving his apprenticeship he attended the Municipal Technical College in Belfast two or three nights a week for three years. Jim Magowan, who worked in James Mackie and Sons, remembers them finishing classes at 9:30 pm and travelling home on the last train to Comber, with John cycling the rest of the journey home.

Punctuality was something he took seriously. He remembered one fellow worker who was always late. One day the boss asked him if he didn't know what time they started in the mornings. He replied that he didn't because they were always started when he arrived!

At that time in Comber there was a cheerful Christian man called Tommy Calvert. He was a bread server and was often about as John was arriving in the town. From his seat on the outside of the bread cart he would shout "Hallelujah, brother". John confessed that, at the beginning, as he rushed for the train at 6:30 am often already soaked through with the rain, it took some effort and much grace to shout 'Hallelujah' back. However, he came to deeply appreciate the encouragement of this older man as he did that of many others who had a profound influence on his life.

One of these was an elder in Ballygowan Presbyterian Church, Mr James Gibson, who was in charge of the Tuesday

Evening Fellowship meetings in that church. He was a wise and discerning spiritual leader. Drawn to John, he took a special interest in him, saw the potential in his young life, gave him opportunities for service, introduced him to other leaders, encouraged and supported him and became a very close and dear friend. John often spoke of the fact that he owed James Gibson an incalculable debt.

After his conversion John started to attend the Fellowship meeting where the addresses were given by guest speakers, many of whom were Belfast City Missionaries. There was a constant emphasis on the high standards for Christian living set out in the New Testament- the limitless power of the exalted Lord Jesus, the ministry of the Holy Spirit, and the call to believers to yield themselves totally to the Saviour, so that they might be cleansed from sin, filled with the Spirit and be daily transformed into the likeness to Christ. John always looked back on those meetings as occasions of learning, challenge and blessing.

Although he was attending the Boys' Brigade in Ballygowan on Monday evening and the Fellowship meeting there on the Tuesday, he was still a member of Kilmood Parish Church. Some time after his conversion he requested the use of the parish hall for evangelistic services on Wednesday evenings. His request was granted and the meetings proved to be very popular. He invited different speakers to give the addresses and the neighbours gathered in increasing numbers. One thing that pleased John was that his mother, who could not get up the steps of the Church in her invalid chair, was able to gain access to the hall. Indeed it was John who usually pushed his mother's chair from their home to the hall. When the hall became unavailable, the meetings were continued in the nearby Drumreagh Orange Hall. It was here that Mr. Harry Geddis, a commercial traveller and a friend of John's, conducted a very successful evangelistic mission. The meetings in the Parish Hall and Orange Hall were graciously blessed by God with some people accepting the Saviour and others being greatly helped. John's efforts and witness were deeply appreciated throughout the neighbourhood as people were aware of his interest in them and especially their spiritual needs.

As a result of his increasing involvement in Ballygowan Presbyterian Church he joined that congregation in 1937. His value was recognized by the minister, Dr William McLernon, who asked him to teach a Sunday School class. For many years Ballygowan was renowned for its flourishing Sunday School work and John felt honoured to be part of that. His class of boys were between 14 and 16 years of age and many were members of the Boys' Brigade company. Recollecting those days many years later John wrote 'The learning of the Shorter Catechism was a matter of great importance and time was spent helping the boys to understand the meanings of the basic doctrines of the Christian faith as set out in the Scriptures and the Catechism. In fact, studying the questions that deal with such matters as the Fall of Man, Repentance, Saving Faith, the Work of the Cross, Justification, Adoption and Sanctification, to mention but a few, helped me as well as the boys to appreciate more fully the implication of those great doctrines for life here and now and their relevance to what lies beyond the here and now'.

German bombers attacked Belfast on Easter Tuesday, 15th April, and on 4th and 5th May, 1941. One consequence of the German air raids was that crowds of residents of the east of the city, many of whom with connections in Ballygowan, flocked over the hills into that district. They came to relatives, friends or whatever accommodation they could find. A member of Ballygowan and a student for the ministry, W M Craig, was asked by Church House officials to assist Dr McLernon. One of his responsibilities was to ensure there was adequate Sunday School provision for the additional children. Three Sunday afternoon district Sunday Schools were already in existence but there was a need for a fourth in the Drumreagh area. Alongside William Craig, John threw himself wholeheartedly into the project. When, in 1943, the former left to become assistant minister in Windsor Presbyterian Church, Belfast, John became Superintendent and held that post until 1946. That Sunday School was much used of God among the local children long after the evacuees had returned home to the city.

While there was much that drew John to Ballygowan, one other 'attraction' was of a very different nature. Agnes Cairns lived in the very heart of Ballygowan village. She was a gentle and attractive girl and as young people John and she fell deeply in love. Although never robust physically, Agnes was to give constant encouragement and devoted support to John, not least through the decisions he had to make in obedience to the Lord's call.

John not only won the respect of people in his district but also at work. Those who worked with him testified that he was an exact, neat, excellent workman. Apparently at one stage he was persuaded to apply for and get a job in Short Brothers and Harland, but he did not stay long. He confessed that he could not tolerate the prevalent attitude to work there. Getting in touch with Harkness's they gladly took him back.

The quality of his discipleship was seen in a test issue in his work. At the beginning of the war, Sunday work, which was almost universally adopted in the time of crisis, was introduced into his firm. John was uneasy about this and he made his opinion known. He eventually reached an agreement whereby he worked some overtime hours during the week and took a substantial cut in his wages in order to have the Lord's Day free for worship, fellowship and service. He was prepared to suffer considerable personal loss for his Christian convictions. Although it was costly for him, he honoured the Lord.

It was becoming evident to many who knew him that here was a gifted, dedicated and deeply sincere Christian man. Before long he was being invited to share in prayer meetings, Gospel meetings, fellowship meetings and open-air meetings in an increasingly wide area. At these he would sing, testify and speak about the Lord. As it became clear that he was destined for some form of Christian service, many people prayed for guidance for him and he himself sought to know God's will for his life. In 1945 he organised a Mission in Drumreagh Orange Hall. He remembered "No-one was converted but I was challenged about my own life".

Soon afterwards he applied to be received as a worker with the Belfast City Mission.

2

BELFAST CITY MISSION

During the early decades of the nineteenth century the population of Belfast grew rapidly as people moved to it from rural areas, attracted by the prospect of employment in the increasingly industrialised town. Many faced unemployment as the local industries could not provide sufficient jobs for the growing workforce. Social deprivation led to increasing crime, vice and drunkenness.

Concerned for the spiritual condition of Belfast's inhabitants, Rev Reuben John Bryce, Principal of the Belfast Academy, supported by other Presbyterian colleagues and friends, formed the 'Belfast Town Mission' in 1827. An undenominational mission, its object was 'the promotion of Christ's cause among the poor, the careless and the churchless'.[1] In 1843 it was reconstituted and linked more closely to the Presbyterian Church. After Belfast was given its Royal Charter raising it to city status, its title was changed in

1895 to the 'Belfast City Mission' and a number of changes were introduced into its organisation. Among its aims were that Mission districts should be co-terminous with the Presbyterian parish areas and a missionary should be attached to each congregation to seek to bring people into a church connection.

By the year 1945 there were some thirty Missionaries on the staff. John submitted his application and in December of that year preached as a candidate for the Mission. He did so at a normal meeting in a Mission Hall which was attended by the Superintendents Board. He took two texts 'The heart is deceitful above all things and desperately wicked' (Jeremiah 17:9) and 'God is love' (I John 4:16). Subsequently, he was accepted and in January 1946 was appointed as missionary in the Donegall Road Hall situated near the rear entrance to the Belfast City Hospital and linked to Elmwood Presbyterian Church.

Since March 1944 Jackson Buick had been working in the City Mission Hall at Ligoniel. He recalls pausing at the entrance to Church House on a Friday morning in January 1945. " A brisk young man approached me enquiring if the Belfast City Mission staff meeting was held there. We both went into that meeting together". It was the beginning of a long friendship with John.

At the beginning John found it a considerable change from living in the country to working full time in Belfast. James Cassidy, the Missionary in Kilburn Street Hall, conducted John round the maze of streets which characterized the area. He confessed that, faced with so many streets, he thought he would never get to know it. But he soon became acquainted with the district and the people in it and was later to acknowledge that "those were some of the happiest days of my life".

When he first came to the Mission he travelled each day from home, so that he would be able to be of some help to his mother. He kept a bike in Comber and another in Belfast so ensuring he would have transport at each end of his journey. Sometimes he would travel by bus instead of train and it was not unknown for him to fall asleep and go past his accustomed stop. After his mother died in 1948 John came to stay in Belfast with his sister Belle and her husband, John Fox, on the Oldpark Road, which certainly eased his burden. They were to provide his home for the next eight years.

John was meticulous in his door-to-door visitation. He was motivated not just by the requirement laid down in the rules of the Mission, but by a heart felt burden for the individuals in those homes who needed Christ. His one ambition was to lead them to the One who had saved and transformed his life. So he gave himself unreservedly to them.

The pattern he adopted in those days in Belfast was one he was to follow all through his life and which bore much fruit.

John travelled around the cobbled streets of the district on his bicycle, stories about which are numerous. On Friday mornings the Mission staff would meet in Church House for a time of prayer and fellowship. After his journey from Comber he would call at Mabel Miller's house and clean his shoes before going to the meeting. On one occasion she drew his attention to the state of the machine, to which he replied "I can't wash that bike, it's only the dirt that holds it together".

Let John himself relate some of his story of those days. "Having been brought up in a rural setting, I experienced some misgivings and even fear as I embarked on the work of knocking doors in the streets of the Donegall Road district, introducing myself as the Belfast City Missionary for that area. However, in a matter of days those fears had evaporated as at almost every door I was greeted with warm friendliness and invited into the homes.

What exciting conversations and discussions took place as I got to know some of the conditions and circumstances that made up the lives of the folk who lived in those streets. There were stories of bereavement occasioned by the effects of the war recently ended-bereavement not only in regard to servicemen and women killed in action, but also those who had become victims of air raids on the city. I met men who had been discharged from the services because of war wounds or impaired health and were no longer able to work; some were resentful and bitter as they felt they had been tossed unto the heap of forgotten things.

Another thing that was playing havoc in many homes and families at that time was the dreaded disease, tuberculosis. I can think of several houses in which two or three and even four members of the family who had fallen foul of that scourge and had been admitted to hospital where they had to remain for six or seven months and in some cases more than a year. Indeed, not a few failed to recover at all, as, for example, a woman of thirty-six years of age who passed away in the City hospital, and in just a few weeks later, her son, sixteen years old, stricken with the same disease, died in Whiteabbey Hospital.

Naturally, those circumstances provided opportunities for the missionary to get close to the families thus affected, showing understanding and sympathy for their plight and giving what practical assistance he could. This opened the door for the sensitive introduction of the Gospel, assuring the people of the love of God for them whatever their circumstances and encouraging them to put their lives as well as their problems into the hands of the Saviour. I saw ample evidence of the power of God to transform individuals and even families as Jesus became real through their simple trust in Him. This did not necessarily change their physical and material circumstances, but their attitude to those circumstances was certainly tempered by the knowledge that God cared for them and gave them the courage and grace to accept whatever might be their lot.

Of course there were homes into which it was difficult to gain access. Sin-perhaps expressing itself differently from today-was no less real, and the message of the Gospel was not

always accepted as the good news it was proclaimed to be. As I engaged in door-to-door visitation, there were some who told me in no uncertain terms that they wanted neither me nor my message. However, being present in the streets and making use of the opportunities for showing care and giving help where possible contributed toward breaking down barriers and even disarming those who were inclined to be hostile.

An interesting and encouraging feature of the work of the Mission in those days was that the Sunday Schools were packed with children. Dedicated teachers were usually forthcoming, and in the main, parents were co-operative in seeing that their children's attendance was reasonably consistent. The annual outing was a great event when five or six buses were required to take the children and parents to Ballywalter or some such place for the day.

In those days attendance at a place of worship on Sunday was observed by many. The Churches in our district were well attended, especially the Evening Service; in fact, the number present at the Evening Services exceeded that at the Morning hour of Worship. Those who came along to the meetings in the Mission Hall were faithful and indeed were instrumental in bringing with them many who had otherwise little interest. One very encouraging aspect of the work in our Hall was the interest shown by men. In particular, we had a weekly 'Men only' meeting when on Friday evenings from 10.00 to 11.00 about two dozen men came together to pray for the blessing of God on the work of the Mission, and I could tell of incidents which I had no doubt were in answer to those prayers.

The television set had yet to become part of the furniture of the home; few of the people in the district had motorcars. In the main they lived in 'kitchen houses'; there were few homes fitted with bathrooms or inside toilets; in many cases the families were too large for the available accommodation and the mother often experienced frustration as she tried to cope with the domestic needs of the family. When the father came home from work-if he was employed- there was little hope of an evening's relaxation in the house because of all the coming and going, and in too many cases he would make his way to the local public house where it was all too easy to become a victim of the drink habit.

In spite of all the physical and material limitations in which the people had to live, there was, nevertheless, a contentment in hearts and homes which is sadly, to a great degree, missing today. True there were families that were broken up because of the irresponsibility of one or both parents; but be it said that in many of those situations the missionary was able to get things sorted out without recourse to any marriage guidance organisation. Divorce was a rarity, homosexuality and lesbianism were terms unknown to the vast majority-there was a standard of ordinary, simple decency in accordance by which most of the people tried to live.

Another thing that used to impress me was the great neighbourliness in the streets. When the front door was opened in the morning, it was customary to leave the key in the outside of the door without concern about it being used by any unwelcome intruder. When trouble of one kind or another happened in a home all the neighbours rallied to the support of that family and that support was given often to the point of sacrifice." [2]

Working in those circumstances John gave himself wholeheartedly to the people of the district he came to love and God greatly blessed his work among them. Full of determination, ability and a capacity for hard work, he made a lasting impression on many in the district. Although his time in the Mission was to be short, he was unsparing in his commitment to both old and young. In turn, he won the love of God's people and even the regard of those who did not agree with him or his message.

In the pulpit he faithfully expounded the Bible and called people to faith in Jesus and over the years saw many from the district respond. John recalled one incident involving one of his work colleagues, a man called Cecil, who was very sceptical of anything to do with Christianity. "One night", remembered John, "as I entered the pulpit in the little hall in Donegall Road, to my amazement I saw Cecil in the congregation. It knocked me off completely in my preaching that night- or so I thought. At the end of the service I went to the door to shake hands with folk as they went out. I wondered what kind of remark might come from my former work mate when he got to the door. He didn't turn up, and when I went back into the hall I found Cecil where I had left him. He was in tears. 'You've got me, John' he said. The 'hard man' who would have had almost communistic leanings, yielded his life to Christ, and that night I shed tears of joy with Cecil".

His pastoral work brought him into contact with all sorts of people. Some were evidently sympathetic to him and the gospel he sought to share. Some were indifferent and others antagonistic. Even with the latter John was not to be put off by any negative response.

On one occasion he went to visit the very sick father of a girl who was active in the Hall. When he entered the bedroom, the man who was far from gospel greedy, swore at him and told him to go to hell. John's response was "No, I am not going there and I'm here to stop you going." The man was shaken by the response. John continued to call at the home and minister to him and by the grace of God he received the Saviour.

Nothing brought him more joy than to lead someone to Christ. Some fifty years later he recalled " When I left the bench I stopped working with things. In the Belfast City Mission I started working with people. I'll never forget the sense of achievement when I built my first cab on a truck. There was a feeling of personal satisfaction and pleasure. I almost felt I had arrived. Nor will I forget the joy and delight I experienced when I led my first person to Christ in the Mission. But there was a difference. In the first case, the pleasure was purely personal; the truck didn't make any response. It mattered not to it whether I had done a good job or otherwise. In the second case, not only was I delighted that I had been the human means of that man's salvation, he too was delighted that he had come. That joy for him and me increased as he started to come to the Hall and took an interest in the Prayer Meeting. But more than that, there was joy in heaven. What had won that man for Christ? He hadn't heard me preach. He had never been inside the Mission Hall. He lived with a wayward son in a dirty little house in Hunter Street. He was 80 years of age. No one cared about him. My visits and those of another Christian showed that lonely old man that there were those who cared about him, and he responded".

John didn't just preach the gospel to people, he lived it out and sometimes that involved giving practical help. When Frank Greenfield's son, Fred, was born, the pram couldn't be wheeled into the house. John learned of their predicament and, using his skills, adapted the bottom step of the stairs to cure the problem. Many have memories of similar acts of practical kindness on his part.

He made himself available to people whoever they were and whenever they needed him. Martin Smyth recalls that in his last year at school he would walk up the Donegall Road around 10:15 pm after an evening's study. Regularly he would meet John cycling up the road and they would chat for a while. One evening John said that he was going to sit with a man who was dying. A week later around the same time they met again and again John told him that he was going to sit with a dying man. "Is he the same man" asked Martin. "No, he got better" was John's reply. The prayers of a righteous man availeth much.

He didn't always get it right. Walter Millar tells of how, not long after he came to work in the Mission, John fell foul of his little sister, Valerie. Coming home one Monday night from the Bible Class with a face like thunder, she stated that she wouldn't be back for, as she said, "He didn't sing my hymn". 'Break Thou the bread of life' happened to be the recognised 'signature tune' for the class and that evening John had decided to sing something else. After a 'public apology' all was well and it never happened again.

He had something of a reputation for not being diverted from his concern for the spiritual welfare of people and it was this that led them to respond to him. On one occasion he noted that some boys were missing from Sunday School. He had an idea where they might be so he walked up to the 'Jampot' (the local snooker hall on the Donegall Road, where 'Hurricane' Higgins started his career). Walking straight in, he called the boys out and marched them down the road into Sunday School.

Not only was he interested in leading souls to Christ but of encouraging them to mature in the faith. That included developing and using their gifts and talents for the Lord. Under his guidance four young men formed a male voice quartet and sang their first piece in the Mission Hall. They were later to be greatly used by God through their testimonies in song in many places.

In the open air work he encouraged those with musical gifts and again gave a lead. Praise bands are nothing new, for the Donegall Road Mission boasted of one in the 1940s. Bertha Scott played the violin, Walter Miller played a piano accordion, and they were accompanied by an electric steel guitar which was played by John himself. Ernie Patterson, who played the fiddle, remembers "I tried to get John to play the fiddle but he didn't take on to it at all."

Along with Sadie Strain, John started a 'sewing class' on Wednesday nights for the young girls in the Hall, and he arranged speakers from different Missionary societies to address them. With that up and running, John was concerned there was nothing for teenage boys.

He and Albert Millar, who was a French polisher, formed a wood-work class. The first project they attempted was a six foot high model lighthouse, consisting of seven interlocking parts. It was part of a dialogue to be performed at the annual Sunday School Social and Prize giving. During the rehearsals Albert's son, Walter, was converted to Christ.

Over the years many other of those young people came to open their lives to Jesus and today are still involved in working for the Master. On John's 80th birthday many of the 'girls' of the mission sent him a birthday card signed in their maiden names. He was thrilled and deeply moved by the gesture.

It was becoming evident to many of John's friends that a wider sphere of work was beckoning him. On one occasion John shared in a funeral with Rev David Porter, a former missionary with the Belfast City Mission and at that time minister of Richview Congregation further up the Donegall Road. David began a friendship with John and was instrumental in being one of those used by the the Holy Spirit to encourage him to begin to think seriously about offering himself for the ministry of the Presbyterian Church in Ireland. John raised with him what he saw as the obstacles in terms of his lack of education as well as the financial implications. However, David persevered and prophetically told John that he would one day be his assistant in Richview!

John's educational limitations meant having to study for matriculation but for two years he persevered. Despite the demanding work of the Hall, which he continued to undertake faithfully, he studied privately and by 1949 had achieved the qualifications to enter Magee Theological College, Londonderry.

His farewell was arranged by the members of the Mission Hall and they made a presentation to him to help him in his studies. However, the Lord was moving in a special way in the Hall and he decided to postpone going to college lest he was outside God's will. He wanted to return the gift but the people would not hear of it. Martin Smyth was going to Magee College that October and coming home one evening his mother told him that Mr. Girvan had called and left him an envelope. On opening it there was a note from John expressing his good wishes, prayerful remembrance and a generous gift to help with his fees-part of John's present.

In October 1950 he finally left the Donegall Road City Mission and headed for Magee, College, Londonderry.

But John did not 'leave' the Belfast City Mission for he was to be linked to it for many years, although in very different roles.

1. S.W. Murray, 'The City Mission Story', Belfast, 1977, p4
2. Belfast City Mission Annual Report, 1995-96, p10

3

COLLEGE DAYS

Training for the ministry of the Presbyterian Church in Ireland involved a six year course of study. Most candidates spent four years at Magee College, Londonderry. In the final terms of their third and fourth years they attended Trinity College, Dublin where, if successful, they graduated at the end of their fourth year. This was followed by two years studying at The Presbyterian College, Belfast (known as Assembly's College, now Union Theological College). Most men beginning that course were about eighteen years old; John was thirty three. Because of his age he could have applied for the concession of a shortened course but he decided to undertake the full course of six years.

His determination was evident right from the start. Most students, especially in their first year, manage to find many other interests to help distract them from their studies. But not John. Robert Crawford, later Professor with the Open

University, who was John's fellow student and room-mate at Magee, recalls another student bending over John's desk on the first night and in an awed whisper saying "you haven't reached line 200 of Virgil already!".

Another kind of impression was made on Brian Moore, who in their first year, shared a room with Robert Crawford and John. On entering the room for the first time, Brian was met by John who bluntly asked him, " What age are you?" "Seventeen", replied Brian. "Well", said John, "I'm twice your age, so you'd better behave yourself!" Despite that introduction, a long and mutually beneficial friendship began between them.

Not only was John somewhat older than his fellow students but he was only too aware that he also lacked their educational advantages. Unlike most of them, he had never attended a grammar school. Knowing he would have to work harder than most in order to achieve what was expected of him, he gave himself assiduously to his studies. Some of them remember how, when they would have been going out to socialise in the evenings, John would have been hard at his studies. Returning late to their lodgings they would find him still at work. His commitment to such long hours of painstaking study took its toll on his physical stamina and often drove him to the point of exhaustion. William Caughey remembers that "his determination and devotion drove him on through difficulties that would have defeated many an average person, but then, John wasn't average". Even under such pressures he adhered rigorously to his principles. For example, while he might study late on Saturday night, when midnight came the books were put away, for he strictly observed the Lord's Day.

His resoluteness was expressed in the little text he had printed and framed and which sat on his desk throughout his student days. It read 'This one thing I do'. A number of years later when addressing another generation of Magee students he encouraged them to follow two principles which he said he had sought to apply in his student days. They were devotion and discipline, which he went on to explain did not just refer to their studies but to their spiritual lives.

His efforts were successful for each year he came first, second or third and regularly won class prizes and scholarships. Eventually he graduated with a Bachelor of Arts degree 'with Respondency' from Trinity College, Dublin, which was in effect a first class degree and the highest he could have achieved.

However, during those student years John's interests were not confined to his studies. He used to say that his student days were even more blessed of God in witnessing than his years in the City Mission.

He adapted well to the College routine and played a full part in student life-academically, socially and in sport. Above all, he was especially involved in the Evangelical Union, a Christian Student body linked with the Inter-Varsity Fellowship, now the Universities and Colleges Christian Fellowship. William Caughey recalls that "we who were members of the Evangelical Union learned much from him at our weekly fellowship meeting. He had a far superior knowledge of the Scriptures and was capable of helping the rest of us in study as well as in other ways". He was elected President and took his responsibilities seriously.

In his first year at Magee he caught a severe bout of influenza but during his illness he and Martin Smyth discussed how best they might use their long vacations. Even though he was indisposed he used the time productively to help plan to bring the Inter-Varsity Fellowship student campaign to Northern Ireland. He became chairman of the organising committee with Martin as Secretary. In 1951 they held a tent Mission on the Donegall Road. In 1952 they worked on the Lisburn Road and the following year in Dee Street off the Newtownards Road in East Belfast.

John may have physically left the Donegall Road Mission Hall but his heart remained with the people there. Although Londonderry and Dublin were far from the Donegall Road, he continued to keep up his contacts. Every night, usually around midnight, he wrote letters to them. As a result, there was a flood of replies which appeared daily in answer to what became known as 'Girvan's letters'.

His pastoral concern for those back in Belfast was extended to his fellow students. Many of them were away from home for the first time and were removed from the normal restraints of home life. As such they were open to all kinds of temptations and influences. John proved to be a friend and counsellor and almost a father to a number of them. Many of his fellow students would seek him out for advice and counsel, but he was not averse to taking the initiative in confronting them about their behaviour. He was ready to go to the point even of telling them, when necessary, that they were growing cold or compromising their evangelical stance. It usually had the desired effect.

John was friendly towards all he met. He despised no-one, even those who would disagree strongly with his theology. He was never reticent about disputing with his fellow students or even his teachers on theological issues and especially on matters that impinged on the Scriptures and on the Person and work of Jesus. At the same time, however hotly the debate developed, he was not one to bear grudges or show disrespect.

On the other hand, he did not suffer fools gladly. One night during a half night of prayer a student spent a long time telling God what he thought of those grieving the Spirit. John's comment was "I don't know about that, but he's grieving me".

He had an apt expression for someone who was annoying him or doing something foolish. He would say 'You are a duffer'. Often he would use it when someone knocked the door of his room. One Saturday afternoon there was a knock and

John called out as usual 'Come in you duffer'. Imagine the shock when the Principal of the College and another dignitary entered. There is no record of the rest of the conversation.

Friendships were forged during those College years which were to last a lifetime. That was true not only of fellow students who went on to serve in the ministry of the Presbyterian Church but of others in the City of Londonderry. One such was T. S. Mooney, a member (later an elder) in Great James Street Presbyterian Church. Encouraged by John T Carson and James Dunlop, 'T S' had started a Crusader Class in Londonderry in November 1930 and his interest in the spiritual needs of young men was extended to the students attending Magee. Among them was John and the two began a long, enduring and productive friendship.

Another friendship which was also to develop later in his ministry was with another businessman, Joseph Goligher, the Secretary of the Christian Workers' Union. 'Uncle Joe', as he was known, was later also to work closely with John during his ministry in Londonderry.

John endeavoured not to show his age and insisted on playing football for the College team in the Derry Thursday league. He was in fact quite a skilful player, but was also noted for his enthusiasm and robustness, leaving his mark on the Presbyterian Ministry in more ways than one!

At least once, his attempts at trying to keep up with the younger men proved almost disastrous. In the early morning he would attempt to race some of the younger students down the stairs to be first at breakfast. However, one morning he tripped on the concrete steps and fell into the hall. As a result he had a kind of seizure and was laid low for a few days. Sensibly he gave up engaging in such races.

Stories of his concern for others abound. When the degree examinations came round most minds were focussed on doing well. On the last day the morning exam paper was on Hebrew and those present were shocked to discover that some fellow students hadn't turned up. They were in lodgings outside Dublin and had thought the paper was to be taken in the afternoon. Understandably, they were greatly dismayed when they arrived at lunch time. John immediately suggested that he would take them to the Professor of Hebrew and ask him to set them a test in the afternoon, which he graciously did. It was a mark of John's concern for others that led him to aid the students, for without his intervention they would probably have had to sit their degree examinations at a later date. But it was also evidence of the regard which members of the faculty had for John. That undoubtedly influenced the professor's decision.

One expression of that respect occurred when John left Magee. He received a letter from R L Marshall, Professor of History and English at the College. In that letter he wrote complimenting John on his dedication to his studies and expressing gratitude for the contribution he had made to College life. He commended him for his forthrightness and the witness of his life and acknowledged the excellent influence he had on his fellow students, as well as recording the esteem in which John was held throughout the college. The letter is somewhat unique in the history of Magee College.

Four years at Magee were followed by two more years at The Presbyterian College, Belfast to complete his theological education. Again, his time there was marked by determination and dedication. Alan Flavelle recalled that John took his studies much more seriously than most other students. On one occasion, when an important examination was coming up, he felt John needed a break. Arriving at John's room at 10 pm to invite him for a game of snooker, he was greeted with John's immediate reaction "Get thee behind me satan!". Alan repeated his invitation several times but all he could get as a reply was " I'm not going and you know I'm not". Nevertheless, he persisted until eventually John gave in, remarking "All right, Flavelle, I'll come, for I know you won't leave unless I go with you."

In 1954 representatives of Magee, Queens University, Belfast and Stranmillis College met to plan the Inter Varsity Fellowship Summer campaign. John was chairing the meeting and after lengthy discussion the time came for different responsibilities to be assigned. He wasted no time looking for volunteers but would look around the room and say "Mr. X, you'll look after the Bible studies" or "Miss Y, you'll take charge of the prayer meetings" and so on. Needless to say it wasn't very democratic, but such was the regard in which he was held that people willingly did as they were asked or perhaps they were too overawed by him that they hadn't the courage to dare to refuse.

During those final years of study students were usually assigned to ministers of large Belfast congregations to be trained in a practical way in the work of the ministry. To John's delight he found himself serving his assistantship in Richview Congregation where his friend Rev David Porter had ministered since 1947. It meant that John was back working in the area he had known from Belfast City Mission days. As well as working in a community he already knew well, he differed somewhat from the usual assistants, having the advantage of a great deal of experience in both preaching and pastoral work.

With typical enthusiasm he gave himself wholeheartedly to the work in Richview as a colleague to David Porter and the Church Sister, Jean McClure. He was involved in the 13th Belfast Company of the Boys' Brigade as a Lieutenant and regularly attended the 13th Old Boys football matches. Richview had a very large Sunday School and John served as Sunday School Superintendent, building up a reserve of teachers he could call on. To help train and encourage those with such an important role he organised Sunday School teachers week-end conferences. These were by no means staid and solemn occasions and often resulted in all kinds of hilarious situations to which John made some contribution.

In his pastoral work he was totally committed to the people of the area. Harold Hughes recalls that John was known to have slept in houses where a family member was near the end of their earthly life so that he would be available to minister to them and the family. He was faithful in his preaching of the Word of God and David Porter reinforced the important lesson that as a minister of the Gospel he was responsible not just to call people to repentance and faith in Jesus but to teach those who had surrendered to Jesus how to live for Him.

Almost all the necessary requirements for entering the ministry had been fulfilled. Before a student is licensed to 'preach the Gospel publically, as a probationer for the ministerial office' he is required to present a 'trial' piece to his presbytery. On 10th April 1956 the Presbytery of Comber met to hear John preach on John 3:16. He was subsequently licensed by the Presbytery on 3rd June 1956 in Ballygowan. At the reception Rev Adam Stewart, speaking on behalf of the congregation, expressed the profound interest with which the members regarded John's welfare. "They were all glad to see him in his present position. It had all been done by hard work...and scholarships had carried the student through the entire six years of his course. At times extreme difficulties had been experienced but he had weathered them all and won through".[1]

With that John waited for the call of God to direct him to the next sphere of labour for the Master. It was not to be a long wait.

1. Newtownards Chronicle, 8th June 1956, p8

4

CARLISLE ROAD, LONDONDERRY

Carlisle Road Presbyterian Church in Londonderry has its origin in a body of people who met in a hall in Fountain Street. After some time they were received into the United Secession Synod in 1837 and the next year their first minister, John McFarland, was ordained. Two years later the Secession Synod and the Synod of Ulster united to form the Presbyterian Church in Ireland.

Its sixth minister was Rev Sam McVicar who had been installed in 1928. During the latter years of his ministry he suffered from ill health and obtained part time assistance from one of the students studying at Magee College, John Girvan, who worked in the congregation from 1952 to 1954. His experience in the Belfast City Mission stood him in good stead and he became well known in the area. Travelling everywhere on his bicycle he would regularly visit in the streets of small houses around the church. Although there was no Boys'

Brigade Company the congregation had a Girls' Brigade Company and John found himself taking the girls for drill! When Sam McVicker retired on 28th July 1956, one of the names considered for the vacancy was that of John Girvan. At the congregational meeting on 16th October a unanimous call was issued to him and he was ordained and installed on 28th November 1956.

The service was conducted by the Moderator of Presbytery, Rev William Steele of First Derry. Revs Adam Stewart of Ballygowan and David Porter of Richview took part and the sermon was preached by Rev George Wynne of Great James Street. In the course of the charge given by Rev William Montgomery, he declared "preaching was not a foolish anachronism or a spent force", [1] words which resonated with John. He went on to make the point that the Christian Church had made headway chiefly though the preaching of the positive Christian message by dedicated personalities. In the providence of God that was to manifest itself in John's life and ministry.

At the congregational reception after the service John bravely admitted that he had not really liked Londonderry while studying at Magee College but this had changed when he came to assist in Carlisle Road Church, so evidently they had made an impression on him just as he had on them. On the same occasion Rev H A Irvine, Professor of Hebrew, New Testament and Biblical Literature in Magee, commending their new minister to the congregation, spoke highly of John's commitment to his studies and in somewhat prophetic vein said that he could forecast a very useful future for Mr. Girvan as minister of Carlisle Road congregation and as a minister of the Presbyterian Church in Ireland.

But John had not come to Londonderry alone. During his years of study he and Agnes had postponed getting married and they decided to do so only when John was ordained. One week before his Installation they were married, on Wednesday 21st November in Ballygowan Presbyterian Church by Rev Adam Stewart. John's best man was Rev Alan Flavelle.

Throughout their years in Carlisle Road, although limited in her involvement, Agnes gave constant encouragement to John in every aspect of Church life. In 1962 her health broke down and she spent fourteen months in hospital. John's own care of Agnes both at home and in hospital was exemplary. Inevitably it took its toll on a man whose commitment to the ministry was marked by a high level of conscientiousness. Looking back he recalled "to go on day by day and keep sane never mind brave was not easy. I did break down one evening in the pulpit. I told Bertie Dickinson I would have to give up. But as I drew on divine resources I kept on". Agnes got some remission in her illness and, of course, would not hear of John even thinking of leaving the ministry to which he was so clearly called of God. He looked after the home, in his words, "at times a bit clumsy" and he appreciated the responsiveness of many in the congregation who would stay with Agnes to allow him the freedom to exercise his ministry.

The congregation had associated with it some 466 families consisting of 1350 people. Along with morning and evening Sunday Schools, Bible Class, Children's Church, it also had a Women's Missionary Association, Women's Fellowship, Junior and Senior Girls Auxiliary, Youth Guild, Junior and Senior Girls' Brigade and Christian Endeavour. With typical enthusiasm John threw himself into regular pastoral visitation of the homes of the people as well as giving his support and encouragement to the leaders and members of the various organisations linked to the congregation.

He soon identified a need in two areas of congregational life. One was the importance of a mid-week meeting. He started this on Wednesdays and used it as an opportunity to instruct people in Bible doctrines. This systematic expository ministry mid-week and also on Sunday evenings was to be a pattern of his ministry in each congregation in which he served. As he preached through a series he proved to be a gifted teacher as well as a unique evangelist. His straight exposition of Biblical books was a significant help to many, especially those young in the faith, enabling them to be grounded in the Scriptures and to face its demands in their Christian lives.

The other area which burdened him was the Church's work among boys. His own experiences of Boys' Brigade had convinced him of the value of such an organisation . In the past there had been a company associated with Carlisle Road but it had ceased to function some time before. In 1957 he raised the subject with the Kirk Session who agreed to revive the company and John offered to serve as Captain until a suitable person would be forthcoming. In the event, he was to remain as both Captain and Chaplain until he left Londonderry seven years later.

He was greatly respected by the boys for his enthusiasm and discipline. On one occasion he came into the hall as the boys were doing physical exercises. Having watched them for a moment or two he went on to the stage and addressed them. "You're like a bunch of old women". Undaunted one boy called out, "Do you think you could do any better?" Even though he was in clerical dress John proceeded to do twenty press ups in front of the company to show how it ought to be done.

His commitment was not just to the weekly meetings of the company but he played a full role at the summer camps where his talks to the boys were memorable. He was always concerned for the welfare of the boys and at a camp in Ballywalter he noticed someone's pyjamas on top of the marquee. He demanded that they be removed to avoid a boy getting his 'death of cold'. His concern for another was ill-conceived for the pyjamas turned out to be his own!

Such was the success of the 3rd Londonderry Company under his influence and direction that a Life Boy Team was started the following year in 1958. For him the provision of a Boys' Brigade Company was not just to fill a gap in a congregation's programme of activities, but he saw it as an opportunity to reach many boys and young men with the gospel. His concern for their spiritual welfare inevitably had an enormous impact on many of their lives.

During his years with the Company, it produced six winners of the Queen's Badge and won the Battalion Bible Class cup on four successive occasions. Such was the regard in which the Company was held that one of John's last engagements in Carlisle Road was in June 1964, when he dedicated company colours, which had been donated anonymously by a group of friends of the company.

John was convinced that one aspect of the Church's witness in the community was to maintain its property in the best possible manner and to provide facilities which would aid in sharing the gospel and for teaching and training people in the Scriptures. It was for that purpose he suggested in 1959 a Renovation Fund with a target of £10,000 and a programme of work on the church property. Although this was a large amount of money in those days in a city plagued with a high level of unemployment, the congregation responded to his leadership. Over the ensuing years through his own enthusiastic leadership the church was reroofed, the stonework restored, the lower rooms refloored and other essential work completed. It also involved Agnes and him moving house from Crawford Square to Clooney Park in 1959.

That particular year was a significant one in the history of Christianity in Ireland for it marked the centenary of the 1859 Revival. The Presbyterian Church in Ireland took specific steps to express its gratitude to God for the outpouring of the Holy

Spirit at that time and for the significant impact on the spiritual life of so many people. As well as a fortnight of mission in Carlisle Road itself in October of that year, John was involved in two other missions - in First Portadown in April and in Trinity, Ahoghill in November. Both were memorable occasions and the beginning of an evangelistic ministry that was to stretch over three decades.

First Portadown was the venue for John's first congregational Mission. In the previous year W P Nicholson, whose crowded missions in the troubled 1920's had had such a profound effect on many lives and communities, revisited Portadown and preached in First Portadown for a week. Following that visit there was much earnest expectant prayer in the congregation in preparation for the mission in 1959. From 12th to 26th April John preached characteristically forthright Biblical messages to increasing numbers of people who attended during the fortnight of evening meetings.

W M Craig recalls that time: "there was a clear sense of the presence of God. John asked those who wished to accept Christ as Saviour to come from their seats up the aisles to where he was standing at the front of the church. It was not an easy indication of their desire, but the Spirit of God was obviously at work. Many of all ages made profession of faith in the Lord Jesus Christ and the majority of them went on to give evidence of transforming grace by their holy walk and ready obedience to the Lord. Of particular interest were some mature men who believed, two of whom were elected as elders very soon afterwards, and others who served in various capacities for many years. Altogether there was a genuineness and wholesomeness about the work that was done. The spiritual level of the congregation was markedly raised." It is not surprising that John was remembered in First Portadown with gratitude and affection.

In his book "If My People" Dr William Fleming describes the events in and around Ahoghill where for some years God had been working in the lives of people, not only in bringing many of them to faith in Christ but of burdening His people to pray and giving them a concern to witness to others. A Mission to mark the centenary of the 1859 Revival was held from 1st to 24th November. It was a united effort between Brookside and Trinity Churches with Rev David Porter in Brookside the first week and John in Trinity the second week. Not only had there been prayer meetings held for weeks before but Rev Fleming had arranged that throughout the Mission there would be one person praying round the clock, day and night for the work. John admitted that he wasn't too sure what he thought about this arrangement but as the Mission went ahead God was evidently at work.

Dr Fleming wrote "God blessed graciously and there were conversions throughout the mission, yet as it drew to a close there was a feeling that there should be a greater response than had been so far. Many of those who had been prayed for and wept over, made no response. The Rev Girvan was requested to extend the mission, and he was able to give two more nights. That closing night will be remembered by the praying people of Ahoghill forever. The presence of God filled the Church and at the close when Rev Girvan made an appeal for those who wished to be saved, to come and stand at the front of the Church, the Church Sexton immediately left his seat at the back of the Church to come to the front. There was an immediate response by men and women from all over the Church who streamed forward. It was deeply moving to see sixteen people of mature years line up across the front. This was God's answer to the prayers of His people". [2]

While John was by no means a controversialist for the sake of it he held strong opinions which were not always appreciated. One incident stands out in his time in Carlisle Road. In January 1961 John, preaching on Temperance, spoke strongly about the provision of strong drink at wedding receptions. He asked "Why should there be strong drink for wedding toasts? Do you realise that the presence of strong drink places some of the wedding guests in an embarrassing position? They don't want to take the stuff but by declining it show their disapproval of it being there and an uneasy atmosphere is created. I enjoy a wedding reception. I enjoy having the chance of expressing good wishes to the young couple but I would very much rather not be invited to a reception in which there is to be strong drink. I would like my congregation to keep that in mind. Drink at weddings may provide the first steps to set young people on the first stages of taking drink". [3]

The report of his words in the press produced something of a furore. It gave rise to sometimes heated correspondence over a period of several weeks in the letters columns of the local newspapers and even further afield, with John being interviewed by BBC television to explain his position. He had to face some criticism but also received support not least from Carlisle Road Kirk Session, the Presbytery of Derry and the Synod of Derry and Omagh.

John held strongly that the Christian position should be one of total abstinence , not only believing that this was the teaching of the Scriptures, but also as the result of his own experience of the ruinous effects of drink on individuals and families. He had a particularly deep concern for young people whom he knew were especially vulnerable and would constantly warn them about being in places where drink was available.

In dealing with individuals John was as forthright. Once when visiting, the door was opened by a woman who had a cigarette in her mouth. Realising who the caller was she quickly snatched it from her lips and put her hand behind her back. Most would have ignored the action but not John who said, "You needn't try to hide it for I can see it".

John firmly believed that his first responsibility was for his own congregation but that did not prevent him from participating in other areas of Christian witness. He was involved, for example, in the Derry Battalion of the Boys' Brigade and the Derry and District Christian Endeavour Union. From 1961 to 1963 he held the post of Evangelistic Convener in the Irish Christian Endeavour Union which meant him giving encouragement to local unions to undertake evangelistic meetings, and reporting these to the Irish Christian Endeavour Council.

He gave his support and encouragement to every effort in the city to share the gospel and develop Christian discipleship such as the Young People's Convention, the 'creation' of John's friend, T S Mooney. Provided it did not infringe on his duties in Carlisle Road, he willingly grasped every opportunity to preach the good news of Jesus Christ when he was able. He often addressed the after Church Sunday evening meetings held under the auspices of the Christian Workers Union in the Guildhall, where Joseph Goligher was Secretary. It was through him that John began another acquaintanceship that was to last the rest of his life. In 1961 the new hospital at Altnagelvin was being opened and John was present. It was there that Joseph introduced him to T B F Thompson and the two quickly became close friends. TBF became one of Northern Ireland's leading industrialists and one year after his conversion in 1947 became President of Garvagh Christian Workers Union. John was a regular speaker at the CWU Hall and occasionally would be called upon to stand in at short notice to conduct meetings.

In March 1963 he was the first minister from Londonderry to speak on the UTV "End of the Day" programme when for a week he faithfully shared the gospel with a wide audience.

Those years in Londonderry were greatly used by God and John saw many lives won for the kingdom. So it was with much regret that the people of Carlisle Road learned in May 1964 that he had received a call to be Minister in Bethany Presbyterian Church, Belfast.

1. Londonderry Sentinel, 29th November 1956
2. William Fleming, 'If My People', Christian Focus, Tain, 1999, p32f
3. Londonderry Sentinel, 25th January 1961

John's mother, Jane.

A later photograph of John's father, James.

John and his sisters, Mary, Jean and Belle.

The youthful John.

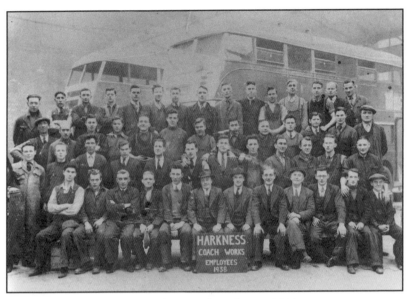

The Employees of Harkness 1938.
(John is fourth from the left in the second row).

1st Ballygowan Boys Brigade Company. (John is the Warrant Officer
third from the right in the front row).

Graduation in Trinity College, Dublin.

The City Missionary.

Licensing in Ballygowan. Rev. S.E.M. Brown, Rev. J.E. Jones, John, James Gibson, Rev. A. Stewart, Rev. J. Cooper.

John and Agnes.

The newly ordained minister.

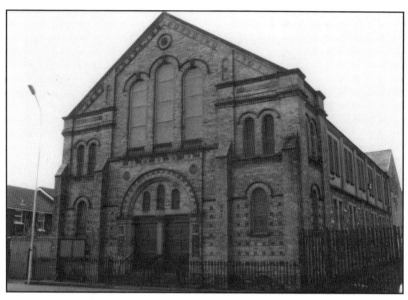

Bethany Presbyterian Church, later Immanuel.
(Photo courtesy of Kevin Harvey).

Carlisle Road Presbyterian
Church.

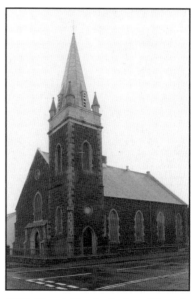

Hill Street Presbyterian Church.
(Photo courtesy of Rodney
McClurg).

John and Mary.

On parade with the 1st Lurgan Company of the Boys Brigade (Hill Street).

About to be Installed as Moderator of the General Assembly.

Irish Christian Endeavour President.

Surrounded by young admirers.

5

BETHANY AND IMMANUEL, BELFAST

The Independent congregation in Agnes Street, Belfast was taken under the care of the General Assembly in 1892 and came to be called Bethany. Rev Samuel Simms was its first minister and he worked there for 40 years. In 1935 he was succeeded by Rev Andrew Crooks who resigned in 1964. When John was installed in Bethany on 30th July 1964 he was only the third minister of the congregation.

When he was leaving Carlisle Road John informed them that "Bethany was not exactly a sinecure and there would be lots of hard work ahead." He was under no illusions about the challenge facing him in ministering to a congregation of some 650 families in a predominantly working class part of the city which had many problems and difficulties. By no means was he daunted at the prospect but immediately and energetically threw himself into the task of becoming acquainted with the congregation and area.

Not used to having a minister wearing robes, the fact that John did caused something of a ripple in the congregation. Soon after John's arrival George Cunningham came as Assistant and frequently they would appear in the pulpit together. In typical Belfast manner and especially among the young people the duo became known as 'Batman and Robin'.

John was a man's man. He once called at a home where the door was opened by the man of the house. On seeing the minister he exclaimed, "She's not in", referring to his wife. John spontaneously responded, "You're a cheeky beggar!". The man was quite shaken by such a response and asked why? John answered "I've come to visit you and you accuse me of being here for your wife". The man laughed heartily and a bond was made.

His straightforwardness was evident in Church as well. One Sunday evening as he was preaching , he stopped and said, "If that couple in the gallery don't come round to the Minister's Room after the service and apologise for their behaviour, I'll be calling with their families this week." When he went back to the Minister's Room after shaking hands with the congregation as they left, he found three couples waiting for him.

It was difficult to get the better of him for he always had an answer and was rarely caught out. John Parkes recalls discussing a Christian Endeavour service with him and suggesting singing a hymn to a new tune. He wasn't too keen on the idea. Trying to persuade him, John Parkes said, "Sure it's the words that are important and not the tune". The unanswerable reply came back "Well, why not sing it to the old tune then?"

The North Belfast Presbytery Visitation of Bethany in 1968 spoke of his faithful pastoral and preaching ministry which was evident in his work in the congregation but also further afield. It referred to the esteem in which he was held by the congregation and the community as testimonies to his work and witness. It goes on to record "His clear thinking and fearless Biblical and evangelistic Ministry have benefitted not only the Congregation but also the Church at large". [1]

The wider Church was benefitting from God's use of his gifts as an evangelist. By now John was in much demand to undertake Missions and each of those he undertook with the approval and the prayerful and practical support of the Kirk Session. This meant him conducting meetings in Richview and Carrickfergus in 1965, Duncairn and St Andrews in 1966, Saintfield Road in 1967, Newington and Ballygowan in 1968 and First Antrim in 1969 among a number of others.

Nor was his ministry confined to Ireland. On Sunday 25th September 1966, he preached at the Youth Service of the Strathpeffer Convention in Ross-shire Scotland. His text was John 3:3 "Except a man be born again, he cannot see the kingdom of God". It was broadcast live on the Scottish Home Service of the BBC and later on the World Service.

His concern was also directed towards Christians and, along with several other Presbyterian ministers, he helped organise a series of rallies. Those involved were WM Craig in First Portadown, Glynn Owen in Berry Street, Belfast, Alan Flavelle in Mourne, Kilkeel and John in Bethany. They were later joined by Martin Smyth in Alexandra and Brian Moore in Albert Street, both in Belfast. People would travel to other churches for a rally when two of the ministers would address the gathering. The meetings were held about three times a year and were intended for the deepening of the spiritual life and the building up of Christians.

At that time there was some consternation among evangelicals in the Presbyterian Church in Ireland about the spiritual life of the denomination and these rallies served as a bond for many of them. It was also a time when all sorts of protests were taking place, with marches and gatherings for many different causes. When he mentioned the rallies to a woman, John was asked by her, "Is this a protest rally?" John replied immediately, "Yes it is. We're protesting against the low level of our Christian living!" Due to the deteriorating security situation these rallies eventually had to be discontinued but during the years when they took place they resulted in much blessing for those who attended and had an impact on the congregations involved.

The fourth anniversary of his installation in Bethany proved to be an unhappy one, for on 30th July 1968 Agnes died while they were on holiday in Newcastle, Co Down. For most of their married life, because of her physical weakness, Agnes had not been as active in Church life as she would have wanted to be. However, she supported John to the limit of her strength. In turn he cared for her thoughtfully, selflessly and with great tenderness. There were times when, in addition to the constant demands of the ministry, he was also housekeeper, cook and nurse to Agnes. Yet never once was he heard to complain or grumble. They had a very special relationship, enriched by their love for and commitment to each other and marked by their united love for the Lord.

John felt most keenly the loss of Agnes. Being the sort of man he was, he wrestled with the enormity of his grief. Alongside this he was unwell and was in constant physical discomfort, relieved only when he underwent surgery. He made a rapid recovery and was soon back at work.

Most of John's ministry in Bethany was exercised in an atmosphere of tension and violence. Although three people had been murdered in the Shankill area in 1966, it was 1969 which witnessed the real outbreak of what has become known as 'The Troubles'. Rioting in Londonderry on 12th August spread to Belfast and other towns. In five days eight people were killed, many injured and many houses and other premises destroyed. Although the Army replaced the Royal Ulster Constabulary and B Specials on the streets, it was not long before tensions again spilled over into violence. During a period of several months John spent many nights on the Shankill Road, where, along with a number of local ministers, he would walk up and down the road speaking to men, and often women, encouraging them to go home and not be involved in the rioting which was almost a nightly occurrence. He was present on the Shankill Road the night the first policeman, Constable Victor Arbuckle was killed by the UVF, an event which had a deep effect on him. Some years later he spoke of this. "We were filled with a sense of horror and shame that such a thing should happen there. Half-a-dozen Churches within a stone's throw of where he died! How could such a thing be! Some of us shed tears that night". He gave himself tirelessly and impressed all who worked alongside him with his physical stamina and emotional courage.

One characteristic of the early days of 'The Troubles' was the eviction of people from their homes by groups belonging to 'the other side'. Late one night a crowd came to force a Roman Catholic family to leave their home in a street off the Crumlin Road. John stood at the front door and confronted the mob. "What are you going to do?" he asked. "We're going to put this family out" came the reply. "Well," he said, "you'll have to get past me first". The men left without touching the family.

On one particular Sunday when almost every other Church had cancelled their evening Service because of the rioting in the area over several nights, John was adamant that, despite the risks, the evening service in Bethany should take place as usual. There were 300 people present!

Many stories are told of his care for people. A bomb exploded causing considerable damage to a number of houses in Landscape Terrace. Learning that some of these were occupied by elderly people, John went straight to Bethany where some young people were meeting and led them off to the houses where, under his direction, they helped tidy up much of the damage. Of course, alongside them, he wielded brush and shovel as well.

In such circumstances John felt compelled to write an open letter to his fellow ministers in the Presbyterian Herald in October 1969. "The charge is frequently made that the Church is not without blame for the troubled situation in which we are living these days, and who would dare to say that there is no truth in the charge? Jesus Christ told His disciples, and as such, all who are really His people, that they are the salt of the earth. The function of salt is to save the mass in which it is from decay and corruption, consequently it would appear that in our Province the salt has lost its savour.

How far are we, as ministers, responsible? Have we been sidetracked from the main issues-declaring dogmatically and on the authority of the Word of God that all men are lost, that men are not fundamentally good but bad, that the heart of man is deceitful above all things and desperately wicked and that there is a Holy God Whom he will one day have to meet in judgment?

Have we proclaimed the Gospel of God's grace against the background of man's fallen condition? That the only hope of salvation lies in a personal acknowledgment of sin, a willingness to turn from that sin and accept Jesus Christ as Saviour and Lord, ever afterwards living out the Christ-life through the power of the indwelling Holy Spirit- in other words, that man's basic need is to be born again?

Or have we been preaching a kind of 'do-it-yourself' salvation-urging on our hearers the principles of the Sermon on the Mount, principles by which it is impossible for an unregenerate man to live? That Sermon was given to the members of the Kingdom of God and it is pointless to ask people to live by the principles of that Kingdom when they are not in it.

Or again, have we got lost in the wilderness of Ecumenical pursuits, forgetting that people as individuals must become living members of the Body of Christ before they can understand what the Bible has to say about the unity of that Body?

However far we as ministers may be responsible for the want of Godly living in the community it is my honest conviction, strengthened by what I have seen and heard in the streets in recent days, that we must ask ourselves whether we are preaching a message that can radically change men's hearts and lives, making them first and foremost children of God, and then really good citizens in the community in which they live.

I am perfectly convinced that the Gospel of the New Testament can do these two things, and I am equally convinced that no power on earth can."

As early as 1965 Bethany Kirk Session were made aware of the Belfast City Council's slum clearance plan which it was thought would affect the area in 1969. In 1970 both Bethany and its neighbouring congregation of Agnes Street, situated almost opposite Bethany Church, were informed of the impending redevelopment of the area and explored the possibilities of union. Since 1946 Rev Donald Gillies had been minister of Agnes Street whose numbers had been steadily decreasing with the movement of population from the area. In the summer of that year both congregations united for services of worship during July and August and this was planned for the following summer. Meantime the debate and discussion continued and by June 1971 both congregations had agreed to unite. Subsequently, Mr. Gillies resigned on 1st October 1971 to become minister of Clifton Street United Presbyterian Church and the congregations were united on 14th October with John being installed as its first minister. Members were asked to put forward possible names for the united congregation and, out of the 20 suggestions received, the name of 'Immanuel' was chosen. At the Kirk Session meeting at which the name was finalised John stated that he would like to see the name on a neon sign in front of the Church. But it never materialized!

He worked sensitively to seek to unite the two groups of people. It did not prove to be an easy task because he had been minister of Bethany at that stage for some seven years and apparently not everyone was happy with every aspect of the union. He had built up relationships in one congregation and now faced the challenge of moulding two congregations into one. The fact that it proved to be a successful 'marriage' was due in no small part to John's tireless efforts to be fair and accommodating.

Although working in a busy parish in Belfast, John's interests were wider than his own congregational life. Although the Disabled Christians' Fellowship existed in England, the first official Committee in Ireland was constituted in 1964 with the first branch being formed in East Belfast in March 1965. In the spring of 1971 John extended an invitation to the Committee of the South Belfast Branch of the Disabled Christians' Fellowship to take a deputation meeting in Bethany. His intention was to have a branch established in North Belfast and this came to fruition in September of that year. He asked permission of the Bethany Kirk Session for the use of the church hall for its monthly meetings. This was readily given and the branch continues to meet there to this day.

There is no doubt that the fact that both his mother and Agnes had suffered from disabilities lay behind his interest and from that time on he was a strong supporter of the Fellowship. He was a regular speaker at many Disabled Christian Fellowship branch meetings and for over 25 years was on its Council of Reference. When the Holiday Home was opened in Newcastle in 1993 it was he who dedicated the complex to the glory of God and for the comfort and happiness of all who would share in its facilities.

Associated with Immanuel congregation was the Jersey Street City Mission and John enjoyed good relationships with the Missionaries, who benefitted from his advice and encouragement. However, at the time they didn't always appreciate his treatment of them.

Denis Bannerman recalls his first Sunday at the Church as the new Jersey Street City Missionary. "It was a Sunday morning in March 1972, when I was sent by an Elder of Immanuel to meet John Girvan. He was preaching and the Assistant, Ivan McKay, was to lead the service - that was the pattern that John adopted with Assistants.

I sat in the minister's room and dutifully waited for the great man to finish a conversation with an Elder - Ivan McKay had already left the room to see to some arrangement for the service. Conversation ended, John turned to me with that infectious and disarming smile for which he was known, and welcomed me with a handshake to Immanuel and to the district. "You'll come into the pulpit with us and I'll introduce you." That frightened me somewhat since I wasn't prepared for that - but I was less prepared for what followed. As we walked the short distance from the minister's room to the door leading into the meetinghouse itself, he turned to and said; "sure you can do the children's address while you are at it." I still don't know how I got through that experience without suffering a heart attack - but I still remember what I used to speak to the children - the fingers on my hand (which no doubt were all shaking). Mind you, I can't remember the point, though I'm sure I found one! When you were in John Girvan's company you needed to be ready for anything".

John continued to have an interest in the wider work of the Belfast City Mission and in 1965 he became a member of the Board of Superintendents and the Governing Body. When in 1972 Rev David Porter, under whom John had served his assistantship in Richview, retired after fifteen years as Honorary Secretary to the Mission, John was appointed to replace him. He was to hold that position until he retired on 20th April 1998, having served for 26 years. Unreservedly, he gave much time and much of himself in fulfilling his responsibilities and proved to be an exceptional inspiration to all in the Mission.

As was the case in other congregations in which he ministered, there was a steady stream of people being converted. They came from a whole variety of backgrounds. Almost immediately they were encouraged to be present at the Midweek Meeting. At this Meeting numbers rarely fell below 100 and were usually much above this figure.

In numerous ways he had a tremendous influence on so many lives and it is significant that during his ministry in Bethany five members of the congregation either entered or began their studies for the ministry of the Presbyterian Church - John Lockington, Noel Williamson, George Simpson, John Parkes and Frank McKeown while Hilary Doherty (nee O'Hara) began her deaconess training.

The union of Bethany and Agnes Street had created a congregation of some 900 families and led John to think seriously about his own ability to maintain the momentum of his ministry for the next number of years. But another factor came under his consideration. By 1972 he had come to the conclusion that it was appropriate that the new congregation should have a minister who had no specific association with either of the former congregations. Other considerations made him amenable to think seriously about another sphere of service. When the Kirk Session met on 25th September 1972 they were shocked to learn from John that he had been approached by the congregation of Hill Street, Lurgan to become its minister. Subsequently, he accepted the call and resigned on 13th November 1972.

As President of the Christian Endeavour Society, he tried his best to be present on the first Sunday of the month for the Consecration meeting. His final Sunday in Immanuel was such a Sunday. The young people had collected together and bought him a wrist watch suitably inscribed. He shed many tears as the gratitude of the young people was expressed and indeed found it difficult to respond to their mark of affection.

At his final Kirk Session meeting in Immanuel they "thanked Mr. Girvan for his untiring work in the congregation, how he had not spared himself in his visiting at the homes and the hospitals, and in the proclamation of the Gospel in clear and certain terms from the pulpit". [2]

1. Minutes of North Belfast Presbytery, 19th November 1968
2. Minutes of Immanuel Kirk Session, 23rd October 1972

6

HILL STREET, LURGAN

Founded in 1684, First Lurgan Presbyterian Church adequately provided for the needs of the town for many years. However, the expansion of the town of Lurgan in the mid nineteenth century, along with the results of the 1859 Revival, necessitated additional accomodation and led to the establishment of Hill Street congregation in 1861. John was installed on 14th November 1972 as its eighth minister in succession to Desmond McConaghy, who had been called to Seaview Presbyterian Church, Belfast.

By now John was highly regarded throughout the Presbyterian Church and other denominations for his strongly held evangelical views and was widely known and specially esteemed as an evangelist. Learning that John had moved from a large Belfast congregation to a smaller one of some 360 families in a provincial town, one wag commented that it was like Bill Shankley, the legendary manager of Liverpool, becoming manager of Glenavon Football Club!

That was not how John viewed himself or his move. He quickly settled into life in Lurgan and immediately gained the respect of many in the congregation and community. He continued to be both an outstanding evangelist and a sound Biblical teacher. The simple truth of the gospel shone through with clarity as did the sincerity with which he proclaimed it. His ministry both in the pulpit and in people's homes was greatly appreciated and they expressed their delight in having him as their minister. That pleasure was increased when they learned of the impending marriage of John to Mary Heyburn, news which was also received with much joy by their wide circle of friends. They were married in Brookside Manse, Ahoghill by Rev Ivan McKay on 23rd January 1973.

Mary was greatly involved in Brookside Presbyterian Church especially among children and young people. Having trained as a teacher, she had taught for ten years in Gracehill Primary School. Giving up teaching she went to Mount Hermon Bible College, London to prepare for work overseas. After a year she applied for service with the Overseas Missionary Fellowship, was accepted, and in March 1968, was commissioned in her home congregation. The preacher at that service was John Girvan. Mary worked for four fruitful years in Taiwan and Malaysia and returned to Ireland in 1972.

Mary had known John during his student days but her first impressions of him were far from happy. As a student at Stranmillis Training College, she was involved in the Inter-Varsity Fellowship student campaign and was to be met at York Street railway station. Much to Mary's chagrin John arrived on his motor bike. As she was wearing a tight skirt she knew she couldn't ride pillion on a motor bike. Noticing her elegance and evident reluctance, John simply commented "Do you mean you won't lower your dignity to ride on the back of a motor bike?" Mary was not amused.

Mary soon endeared herself to the congregation of Hill Street and became greatly involved in the life of the congregation. She was not only a wife and home-maker but a confidante, encourager and prayer partner, supporting John in every aspect of his ministry. She was not averse to providing him with constructive criticism, which he confessed he didn't always want to hear, but always benefitted from it.

Mary's experience in Taiwan proved to be providential. When the War in Vietnam ended in 1975 many Vietnamese refused to stay. Thousands fled in leaky boats and became known as the 'boat people'. Many of those who survived the horrors of the journey to the Gulf of Thailand found refuge in other countries. In 1979 Britain took some 10,000 and a number of families found homes in Craigavon. Because of her ability to speak Mandarin, Mary was asked to assist in providing educational facilities for adults and children. She readily responded, and through her warm personality and willingness to put herself at their disposal, made a lasting impression on those whom she helped. Eventually, after two years, when John was elected Moderator, she felt she wanted to give him her full time support and so relinquished the work which she really loved doing.

Like many other towns in Northern Ireland, Lurgan did not escape from terrorist activity. During John's ministry several bombings affected the homes or premises of members of the congregation. Not only did he turn up to give moral and spiritual help, but he and Mary came in working clothes prepared to give a hand with the physical clearing up, even bringing their own equipment to do the job.

In 1975 a Roman Catholic resident of Hill Street was shot by the UVF at his home only yards from the Church. It was not easy for John to visit the family but his presence in that home was much appreciated. This was only one of many instances where he ministered in very difficult situations.

John became a member of the General Assembly's Irish Mission Committee in 1973 and in 1978 became its Convener. His contribution was summarized in the tribute paid to him in the General Assembly's Reports for 1983 when he retired from the convenership. It reads "When appointed Convener of the Irish Mission Committee Dr John Girvan brought to this office not only his experience as a parish minister but his wider and mature experience as an Evangelist known and proved throughout our Church. His vision and concern to lead people to a real and meaningful faith in Christ found an affinity with the aims and principles of the Irish Mission. This was reflected by the fact that in his Moderatorial year he took as his theme 'Ireland for Christ'.

As Chairman of the Committee his positive, gracious and firm handling of the business was much appreciated by all the Members. His ready wit and sense of humour, plus his cheerful attitude added much to the friendly atmosphere and sense of fellowship which prevailed in all our meetings. Sincere gratitude and thanks are expressed to Dr Girvan for his devotion, work and service to the Irish Mission over the past five years."

John continued to be involved in congregational missions. He preached in Anahilt, Dromore, Drumbo, Drumgooland, Carland and Newmills, Clough and Seaforde, Westbourne, Stewartstown, Brigh and Albany among others and God blessed his ministry through the conversion of many to Christ. Appreciating how much John was in demand, the congregation gave whatever support they could both prayerfully and practically. One example of the latter was that Billy Duff arranged for a number of members who would take turns to drive John to various meetings, so easing his burden, something that John deeply appreciated.

One such mission he spoke at was in Molesworth Street, Cookstown from 15th to 29th January 1978 with Eric Black of First Portadown as song leader and soloist. Trevor Coburn, then minister, recorded the events." It must be confessed that it was with great trepidation and little faith that we approached the time of mission; but on the first night four hundred people were present and the mission got off to a promising start. Attendances held up during that week. That is, until Thursday night when a bomb exploded at premises in the Main Street end of Molesworth Street, not far from where Molesworth Church was situated. However, the incident only affected the attendance on that evening-though the meeting itself went on. By the middle Sunday, numbers had increased to six hundred. They continued to rise during the second week and on the concluding Sunday we had to put one hundred and fifty extra chairs into the Church to seat the eight hundred people present.

Initially our thoughts were that the mission was intended primarily for members of Molesworth congregation; but there was a certain amount of outside publicity and it was hoped that others would come along. Here again, things happened in a remarkable way; denominational barriers were broken down and, in the end, it mattered not which Church we belonged to, for in the truest sense of the text we were, indeed, 'all one in Christ'.

It was evident from the commencement that God was moving in the hearts and lives of young and old. Eric Black's solos were a message in themselves and his leading of the community singing beforehand was an inspiration and a blessing to many. Mr. Girvan's challenging presentation of the gospel was simple and plain yet gracious and telling. In preaching the good news of the gospel he preached 'Christ and Him crucified'. He described what God in His free and undeserved love had done for the salvation of sinners. The offer of forgiveness of sins and of personal salvation and the warning of the future judgment were all touched on. It was made clear that a response was demanded for the gospel was to be received, Jesus Christ was to be believed in, and the gift of eternal life was to be accepted. We needed to repent and turn from sin; and we needed to believe and turn to God. As the nights passed it became obvious that God was stepping in in a mighty way. About sixty people confessed to have committed their lives to Jesus Christ; this included people of all ages, some children, but mostly adults right up to a man of eighty-one. It included people of a wide range of occupation, the housewife, the professional, the farmer, the businessman. It included some married couples; but the interesting thing was sometimes the wife or the husband came first, to be followed a few days or a week or so later by the other partner. Those who were opposed to the very idea of a mission came to see what was happening and were won by the love and grace of God.

As a result of the Mission larger attendances were seen at evening services and the midweek meeting for prayer and Bible Study. Indeed, the mission meant a lot to the Christians and created a wonderful unity and fellowship among them and transformed the spirit of prayer. Over the years the 1978 mission has never been forgotten and we thank God for His agent and missioner, the Rev John Girvan. We had seen God at work and those who were privileged to be there and to have taken part in it felt very humble and to God we give the praise and the glory".

Of a different nature was his involvement back in North Belfast in the spring of 1976. In 1975 the North Belfast Presbytery discussed the possibility of an outreach to men. Eventually this became known as North Belfast Outreach targeting industry, clubs and schools. It was to be led by Martin

Higginbottom and Bob Spratt. However, on the eve of the outreach the former was injured in a road accident and had to withdraw. The main burden for the meetings in industry was taken over by Bob Spratt assisted by John and a number of other ministers who were also involved with clubs and schools. They were well received in the 28 firms which were visited and they dealt with requests for almost 750 Testaments.

During the 1950's and 1960's there was a lack of good evangelical literature available for Christian people. Concerned about this, a group of ministers and elders of the Presbyterian Church in Ireland came together to form 'The Presbyterian Fellowship'. They encouraged one another and others to write material which would help Christians in their understanding and practice. Over a period of years they were to produce booklets on a range of subjects such as the Westminster Confession of Faith, Presbyterian Worship, Baptism, the Lord's Supper, marriage, as well as Bible Study guides.

John had written a little leaflet which he used in missions he was conducting. In the mid 1970's the Presbyterian Fellowship approached him to offer to publish it for him. A short and simple explanation of the gospel, it was produced as a booklet entitled "Salvation, How?" It was reprinted several times and over the last number of years has undergone several reprints by the Irish Mission with a different cover and the Bible references changed to the New International Version. Not only did John himself continue to use it but over many years it has been used by others who have conducted Missions as well as individual Christians seeking to provide people with a clear and simple presentation of the gospel. [1]

Not only was he concerned for the salvation of members of his own congregation but he had a burden for the people of the town and the surrounding area. His popularity was evident throughout the town, but John never sought to capitalise on that to the detriment of other congregations. Instead he encouraged his brother ministers and desired to build up other congregations as well as his own. He was a unifying force among local congregations and won the respect of many in other churches for his evangelical zeal. This was evidenced in his Chairmanship of the Lurgan United Convention and, when plans were suggested for a 'Way to Life' Crusade to be led by Dick Saunders in 1976, John was the automatic choice as chairman of the organising committee. Not only was he responsible for guiding them through all the meetings in preparation for the outreach, but gave practical help at every level, even to the extent of physically helping to put up the tent in the grounds of the Junior High School.

His interest in young people encouraged him to restart the Senior section of the Boys' Brigade to supplement the Junior Section already in existence. Although he was very much a Boys' Brigade man, this did not mean he acted to the detriment of the Scout troop but did all he could to encourage their work among young people. A Junior Christian Endeavour had been running for some years and in 1976 a Young People's Christian Endeavour was formed with Mary taking a leading role. In 1979 a crèche was begun during the Sunday morning service.

From time to time John would take a group of young men and teenagers and train them by helping them pray and lead and speak and then would encourage them through Christian Endeavour to use those gifts he had discerned they had. In addition he gave great support and encouragement to those who felt called by God into 'full time' Christian work. During his ministry in Hill Street Geoffrey Jones went to Bible College and eventually into the Presbyterian Ministry and Elizabeth Matthews became a Woman Worker, Deaconess and later Missionary in India.

That interest in young people and children led him to engage with them in different activities, but not always with beneficial results. On a Youth Club outing to Castlewellan Country Park he became involved in a football match. Suddenly, he was seen to limp off and, along with Mary, make his way to his car. They gave no explanation and no-one knew why they were leaving, but it transpired that he had broken his ankle. Despite being in plaster for several weeks it didn't slow him down or keep him out of the pulpit, although he discovered that his footballing days were over.

The congregational property included the McClure Halls which had been opened in 1958. During John's ministry it became clear that additional accommodation was needed but there was no room to expand outwards. Eventually it was decided to build upwards and a new suite of two storey halls were built and opened on 18th October 1978 at a cost of some £60,000.

On 13th April 1980 he paid a nostalgic visit back to Ballygowan to preach at the 50th Anniversary service of Ist Ballygowan Boys' Brigade Company. However, other events that year made it a significant year for him.

In both his previous congregations as in Hill Street John had an active interest in Christian Endeavour. Over the years he given much encouragement not only to the local Societies but at District level as well. As a mark of the esteem in which he was held, he was chosen as Irish Christian Endeavour Vice President in 1978, President designate in 1979 and took office as President in September 1980.

In his Presidential address at the Installation service in West Presbyterian Church, Ballymena , John emphasized the importance of witnessing among young people and also remarked upon the resurgence of interest in the Christian Endeavour Movement in Ireland. "It was important", he said, "to be awake to the desperate needs of today with such disillusionment and despondency among people. We should always recognise, however, two great resources at our disposal, namely the aid of the Holy Spirit dwelling within us, and the power of prayer in our lives".

In the course of his duties as President he visited Belfast, Bangor, Newtownards, Portadown, Dublin, Central Ireland (where the gathering was at Cloughjordan in Co. Tipperary), Enniskillen, Londonderry, Ballymena, Carrickfergus and Glengormley as well as a number of other places.

1981 was the Centenary Year of World-wide Christian Endeavour, and John presided at the opening of the Convention in the September of that year which celebrated the fact. By this time he had been elected Moderator of the General Assembly and so from June to September 1981 Irish Christian Endeavour had a Moderator as President- a somewhat unique occurrence.

In September 1980 he was part of the delegation from the Presbyterian Church in Ireland to the Eastern Area Council of the World Alliance of Reformed Churches meetings held in Brasov, Romania. During their time there John had the opportunity to meet a number of pastors in the villages between Brasov and Cluj. He was deeply impressed by the spiritual depth and vital witness of many who were suffering persecution under the communist regime of Nicolae Ceausescu. What also deeply moved him was the singing at the services and the kindness of people who, although quite poor, wanted to give gifts to their western friends.

On the last day of the visit another delegate, Tom Scott, and John found themselves in some shops in Bucharest spending the last of their currency which they were unable to take home with them. In one shop John picked up a tin whistle and began to play ' The Sash my father wore'. When he had finished the lady serving at the counter told him how wonderful it was. John's reply was " I could give you the words too- it is old but it is beautiful".

For many years John had been a regular attender at the the Portstewart Convention. Although not a member of the

Committee he was responsible over a considerable number of years for the open air meetings which were held at the harbour each night, weather permitting. In June 1982 he was one of the speakers, giving two evening addresses as well as speaking at the missionary reception.

In April 1984 John indicated his intention of retiring at the end of the year. He expressed his desire to have one last mission in Hill Street before his ministry ended. In agreeing to his suggestion the Kirk Session asked him to conduct it himself. So from Sunday 21st to Saturday 27th October 1984 he preached with typical fervency and directness. Subsequently the Kirk Session recorded in their minutes the following comments. "There was unanimous agreement this had been a week when the presence of the Holy Spirit had been very evident, many had come to know the Lord Jesus as Saviour and the spiritual life of the congregation had been deepened." It goes on "the preaching of Dr. Girvan was of the utmost importance, reference being made to his liberal use of scripture in every sermon and to his sincerity and concern which established the tone of the whole series of meetings". [2]

On the 13th January 1985, exactly 39 years to the day when he started as a Belfast City missionary, he preached his farewell sermons in Hill Street.

1. Appendix A, page 115
2. Minutes of the Hill Street Kirk Session, 9th November 1984

7

MODERATOR OF THE GENERAL ASSEMBLY 1981-2

Each year in the Presbyterian Church in Ireland a minister is chosen by a Presbytery to serve as its Moderator for a twelve month period. This is usually arranged in such a way that each minister takes their turn unless they ask to be excused. In 1962 John had served as Moderator in the Derry Presbytery. In the Armagh Presbytery to which Hill Street congregation belongs this election is normally by order of arrival in the Presbytery and in March 1980 John took up this office and served the Presbytery with his usual efficiency. Before he handed on responsibility to his successor in March 1981 he had been given an even greater honour and entrusted with exceptional responsibility.

At the February meeting of the Presbyteries each nominates a minister to serve as Moderator of the General Assembly for the ensuing year. When the (then 22) Presbyteries met in February 1981 John Girvan won the support of eight

Presbyteries and was nominated as Moderator to take up office in June. He admitted to a newspaper reporter that he was 'overwhelmed' by his election. With typical modesty he confessed "I knew my name was being talked about but I certainly did not feel that I would rise to that height". Like many others before and since who have been called to that office, he faced it with a deep awareness of the privilege he had been given and yet much apprehension at the responsibility entrusted to him.

His year of office coincided with the International Year of Disabled People, an issue that lay close to his heart. It was appropriate then that at the Moderator's Rally on the Wednesday night of Assembly week John should include in the programme John Montgomery, a missionary with the Belfast City Mission for 30 years, seventeen of which he had been blind, and Emma Good, a twelve year old neighbour in Lurgan who daily travelled to Fleming Fulton School in Belfast.

John chaired the meetings of the General Assembly with firmness and tact and at moments of tension his ready wit was evident. An invitation had been extended to the Archbishop of Canterbury, Dr Robert Runcie, to address the Assembly. This did not meet with universal approval and in fact some 78 members of Assembly recorded their dissent from the decision. It was rumoured that there would be a walk-out protest. Before the Archbishop's speech one member rose to allege that a threat had been made against him if he involved himself in such action. From the floor of the Assembly he asked the Moderator "What is the position when a member of this Assembly is threatened with physical violence by another member on behalf of several others?" To an outburst of laughter, the Moderator replied "Take it to the Lord in prayer". "That was a serious question" the speaker said, to which John retorted "That was a serious answer".

Another controversial issue was the proposal not to send any Presbyterian representatives to meet the Pope on his proposed visit to Britain in May the following year. It was passed by only eight votes, but it was something of a relief to John who admitted that he would not have led such a delegation if they had been appointed.

Such controversies were not confined to the meeting of the General Assembly. From the beginning John had made it clear that he would not be attending the regular monthly meetings of the four Church leaders which included the Roman Catholic Cardinal Tomas O'Fiaich. He did so out of the conviction that because there were major doctrinal differences between Presbyterianism and Roman Catholicism he did not want to be drawn into the 'ecumenical dialogue' which a number in the Presbyterian Church in Ireland were advocating and encouraging. John also had strong reservations about the stance taken by the Cardinal over the Hunger Strike in the Maze prison. Even so, he went to meet the Cardinal in a private capacity to explain his position. They had a friendly chat, drank coffee and the Cardinal invited him back at any time. One of John's friends made the comment. "Typically Irish. John went to meet the Cardinal to tell him he wasn't going to meet him!!"

A Christmas Carol service had been organized by the East Belfast Community Council in St. Anne's Cathedral as a 'Service of Reconciliation'. The leaders of the four main Churches were invited, but John refused to take part. He explained "I declined to be involved in a joint act of worship with the Roman Catholic Church because it could give the impression that fundamentally we are agreed on matters theological, when in fact we are not. This does not mean, however, that I do not extend the hand of friendship to all sections of the community".

But he had also explained that, if he felt that special circumstances warranted it, he was prepared to meet with the others to discuss particular issues. So it was that in April 1982 John went along with the other three Church leaders to meet the Secretary of State, Mr James Prior, to express concern over rising levels of unemployment. Of course some parts of the press sought to sensationalise it. One report of the meeting was under the banner headline 'O'Fiaich and Girvan unite in deputation over unemployment'.

John's year in office covered one of the most difficult periods of the Troubles. The Hunger Strike was at its height. The first to die was Bobby Sands in May 1981 and nine others were to follow until October when the strike was called off. It was a period of great community violence and tension. Some 100 people were killed including 16 members of the Royal Ulster Constabulary and the Royal Ulster Constabulary Reserve, 9 members of the Ulster Defence Regiment and 9 soldiers along with 50 civilians and 16 terrorists.

There were many terrorist incidents which affected a number of congregations and even Presbyterian headquarters did not escape. At around 2:15 pm on Saturday 22nd August 1981 a bomb in a car, parked in the Wellington Street alley at the side of Church House, Belfast, exploded. The force of the blast from 300 pounds of explosives blew a hole in the stonework and demolished some roofs. Windows were smashed, several rooms, including the Moderators' Room, the Board Room, the Presbyterian Women's Association office and the caretaker's flat, were wrecked and the Assembly Hall organ was extensively damaged. Eventually the repairs were to cost almost half a million pounds. Not only did John immediately make his way to the scene, but took off his coat and got involved in the clean-up operation to make the building secure.

Certainly John was unequivocal in his stand against terrorism. In his capacity as Moderator, John attended the funerals of several Presbyterian members of the security forces killed while on duty. Speaking in Comber at the funeral of

Stuart John Montgomery, a 19 year old RUC man killed in Pomeroy on his first police patrol, John admitted that he had hoped to speak without rancour but there were certain things that needed to be said to those who perpetrated such acts. He continued "It is God who has given life and the person who destroys the life of a fellowman is guilty of the worst crime he can possibly commit, and God will hold him responsible.... The Bible states that the fate of the unrepentant murderer is to have a place in the lake which burns with fire and brimstone and this is not a temporary punishment... Let me say to you whose hands are stained with the blood of a fellowman: You may escape punishment for your evil deeds in this world but what about that God-given conscience with which you have got to live. At any rate there is no escaping that great day of reckoning when you will be face-to-face with the One who regards human life as sacred, and to Him you will have to give account. Nor will it be of any help then for you to say you were a member of an organization and had to carry out your orders. Today you may hide your personal identity in membership of such an organization but on that day you will stand dreadfully alone and no prayers offered for you then will be any avail. I suppose if apprehended, brought before the courts, found guilty and sentenced, you will immediately ask for special category treatment. How dare you ask for special concessions? It would be totally unjust for any such concessions to be granted.

I am a preacher of the Gospel of God's grace and I must tell you that God's salvation is available for you. But to have that salvation you must confess your crime of murder to God and to the civil courts, and sincerely repent of that crime. It is my prayer that you do so."

Among the many terrorist related deaths was the brutal murder of Rev Robert Bradford on 14th November. The Ulster Unionist MP for South Belfast had been holding his Saturday political surgery at a community centre in Finaghy when he was shot several times at his desk. Also to die in the attack was the caretaker, Kenneth Campbell. The days following Robert Bradford's death and funeral were extremely tense and feelings in loyalist areas were running very high. The Secretary of State, James Prior, who had to be rescued by bodyguards from being attacked at the funeral, wrote of monitoring events from RUC headquarters and commented, "As we sat there we could not be sure whether emotions would boil over and the whole province become indeed ungovernable. It is not an experience I would ever wish to live through again". [1] Along with many others John worked to seek to bring a word from God to people and to try to reduce the tension in the country.

In the aftermath of the murders Protestants made plans for a 'Day of Action' on Monday 23rd November, when thousands of people gathered at different venues to protest against the British Government's security and political policies. Consequently, John called the Presbyterian Church to a Day of Prayer on Sunday 22nd and he himself was greatly heartened by the response throughout the Church, believing that the Lord worked to ease the tension which was extrememly high across the community.

On that Monday he led a delegation to meet with James Prior. John records that they went "to tell Mr. Prior that the people's confidence in the government and the security forces was at its lowest and to urge the government to take effective measures to root out terrorism. Many of our people are living in real fear, we said, fear of their very lives. Small Protestant enclaves are surrounded by IRA members, and we know of farmers too afraid to go into their fields, while others have been intimidated off their lands.

We told Mr. Prior that there are too many unresolved murders, and our people genuinely feel that the IRA are winning this war. They believe that the feelings of Roman Catholics are more respected than theirs. They are seized with hopelessness bordering on despair. We feel that government policy is wrong and that the government is more concerned about international opinion than in beating the terrorists."

The Secretary of State was evidently left in no doubt as to the feelings of most Presbyterians.

On Saturday 28th November 1981 Rev Dr Ian Paisley addressed a rally in Glasgow , during which he declared that IRA terrorists "had better watch out because we are there to murder or kill them before they murder the Protestants". John responded by describing such comments as 'non-Christian'. He said "murder is murder from whatever source it comes and I would encourage our people not to be led by anyone along that road at all. It is a road that leads to hopelessness." [2] Dr Paisley's response was to denounce John. However, in the event, John did receive much support both from within and outside PCI.

BBC Radio tried to have a 'head to head' discussion between John and Dr Paisley on its Sunday Sequence programme but the former refused, commenting, "I have no desire to get into a tangle with anybody. I have made my statement and I have nothing to add or take away from it".

Despite these rather depressing events John and Mary enjoyed a year full of engagements, both in Ireland and on their visit to Malawi. On 29th July, as the world watched the wedding of Prince Charles and Lady Diana Spencer, John and Mary arrived in Blantyre. They found the airport covered in national flags and the VIP lounge to which they were escorted was fragrant with the scent of beautiful flowers. John couldn't resist commenting "How lovely for you to do all this for us". "Well actually", one of their African hosts replied, "the President of our country left here two days ago to attend the Royal Wedding".

One incident in that visit to Malawi typifies his practical concern. In Livingstonia they spent some time with Freda Algie, who worked among the women of the villages. Discovering that she was greatly hampered by lack of transport, on their return to Ireland they set about raising money for a suitable vehicle for Freda, which proved to be a great asset to her and her work for a number of years.

His long association with and regard for the work of the Belfast City Mission led him to ensure that he managed to visit every Hall during his Moderatorial year. In every place he was received with great warmth and brought much encouragement to the workers he met.

John was in his element meeting people but it did not always work out as he would have wished. Ivan McKay recalls an incident when John attended the General Assembly of the Church of Scotland. "We were entering Holyrood Palace when he approached a guard in a sentry box with the question 'Laddie, where are you from?'. The guard stared straight ahead in total silence! John - on the one and only time I saw him slightly embarrassed - came away and laughingly said 'the wee blighter wouldn't speak to me!'."

One feature of his year in office was the organising of a rally in each of the Presbyteries at which he spoke on the subject of revival. He commented that not only were they well attended but there was evidently "a deep longing for an outpouring of the Holy Spirit in terms of revival blessing, resulting in a higher quality of Christian living and the genuine conversion of those who are, as yet, uncommitted to Christ."

John took special delight in being given the opportunity to preach the gospel all over Ireland, something he did with his usual clarity and faithfulness. Among his many engagements that year he undertook a fortnight mission in the congregations of Garmany's Grove and McKelvey's Grove, with a week spent in each of these congregations situated in County Monaghan. His official title may have been that of 'Moderator of the General Assembly' but during that year he remained 'John the evangelist' and his ministry touched many lives throughout Ireland and beyond its shores.

1. Quoted by D McKittrick, S Kelters, B Feeney and C Thornton, 'Lost Lives', Mainstream Publishing Company Ltd., Edinburgh, 1999, p 887

2. Belfast News Letter, 30th November 1981

8

RETIREMENT AND LAST YEARS

Once he had decided to retire, with the assistance of members of their family circle, John worked hard at preparing their retirement bungalow in Bangor, Co Down. Mary admits that she had the ideas and John carried them out. Using skills he had learned as a young man he made several items of furniture with his own hands.

Soon after they made their home in Bangor, Rodney Sterritt, minister of Greenwell Street, Newtownards, approached John to enquire if he would like to help out in his large and busy congregation by doing some pastoral work. After some consideration John agreed and started working in the congregation in the spring of 1985. So began a link with that congregation for the next seventeen years.

It wasn't long before he and Mary discovered one of the bonuses of their association with Greenwell Street when they had the pleasure of linking up with members of their family circle and with people who had connections with Ballygowan.

John preached once a month and spoke regularly at various groups in the congregation, with a special interest in the Men's Fellowship. However, his responsibilities were mostly in the realm of district visitation, an aspect of the ministry he loved and into which he entered with enthusiasm. He often said "more people come to the Lord at their own fireside than anywhere else". As he got to know people so they got to know him and, as in other places, his love for people was very evident.

The general attitude to him is summed up in two comments. One elderly woman said " I love to see Dr Girvan coming, he does my heart good." Another man, whom John believed to be 'not far from the kingdom' commented, "That man Girvan doesn't beat about the bush."

But he didn't always meet with success. Calling at a house one evening, the elderly lady who answered the door said, "Oh, Dr Girvan it's great to see you, but could you please call back, for there's a big wedding on in Coronation Street and I would love to see it." The fact that the wedding was preferred before him caused him great amusement.

During his time with Greenwell Street, he was not only a loyal colleague to the minister but proved a valuable help to the Ordained Assistants who served in the congregation. They all benefitted greatly from his advice and encouragement.

When Rodney Sterritt was elected Moderator of the General Assembly in 1991 it was natural for John to take charge of the congregation. It wasn't in his character to be merely a stop gap for a year but he gave himself fully to the life and work of the congregation. As it turned out, this included supervising the appointment of new organist, a Boys' Brigade captain and a caretaker.

Those years were to bring their joys and sorrows. One such involved TBF Thompson. In July 1986 Kathleen Thompson, TBF's wife died. As his close friend, John could empathise so readily with him and spoke at her funeral service with great warmth and gratitude for a faithful servant of the Lord. Her memory is perpetuated by the TBF Thompson Ministries Headquarters in Garvagh, which was dedicated by John on 1st November 1986. When four years later TBF was to marry Betty Kelly, John was his best man and Mary, matron of honour.

Although involved with Greenwell Street, John was to a large extent freed from ordinary congregational duties and he readily responded to invitations to undertake missions in many congregations. A list of some of these provides an indication of his widespread ministry of evangelism. In 1985 he conducted missions in Ballyroney, Drumlee, Glendermott, First Carrickfergus, Kilkeel and Carnmoney. 1986 saw him in Newbliss, Glenarm, Carnalbana, Moy, Gardenmore, Newtownstewart. The following year he preached at missions in Clones, Stonebridge, Ballyhobridge, Cullybackey, Sandys Street and Downshire Road. He conducted missions in 1988 in Banbridge Road, Cavan, First Cookstown and Second Donegore. In the following years, for example, he preached in First Kilrea, Third Portglenone, Bellasis, Ballyalbany, St. Johnston and Ballylennon. In many ways those were golden years and God richly blessed many lives through his ministry.

For most of his life John had enjoyed excellent health but in 1990, when he and Mary were on holiday in the West of Ireland, he became seriously ill. Mary promptly drove him directly to the Belfast City Hospital. When a close friend called to see him John said "If God is saying to me 'It's quitting time' I'm happy to go. He has given me a good long day to work". But it wasn't. After major surgery he recovered quickly and was back into his retirement programme of meetings and missions.

The regard with which he was held as an evangelist by many led him to be invited to conduct a seminar on Personal Evangelism held in Dublin in September 1992 under the auspices of the Irish Lausanne Council for Evangelization.

His association with the Boys' Brigade continued. For some time John had shared with a number of other ex Boys' Brigade members a concern about the direction of the Old Boys' Association, believing it to be primarily interested in sporting activities. In 1983, the Centenary Year of the Boys' Brigade, The Steadfast Association had been formed in England. Launched in the Royal Albert Hall, its object is 'To further the Object of the Boys' Brigade and to foster the spirit of comradeship between past and present members of the Brigade and to render service to others'. Such an organization which enables Old Boys and supporters to keep in touch with The Boys' Brigade and to provide practical support and assistance was close to John's heart. In the early 1990's some men in Ireland considered forming a local branch of the Association. This they did and when they met in 1992 they invited John to become its first President, an office he held until his death. He certainly was more than a figurehead for he played a very active role in the committee and association meetings.

In the 1960s a number of evangelical ministers in the Presbyterian Church in Ireland met regularly for mutual encouragement and Bible study. The venue was usually Alexandra Presbyterian Church, Belfast. Out of that 'Minister's Conference' developed the 'Westminster Fellowship' which was established in 1974 with similar aims. John was a member of the original Conference and was elected its Chairman in 1972. In both groupings he played a significant leadership role and personally provided much encouragement and helpful advice especially to younger ministers. Held in the highest regard by those of all ages, many benefitted immensely from his experience and wisdom which was always shared with openness and humility and out of real concern for his brethren in the ministry. This he achieved not only through personal contact but through those memorable occasions on which he addressed meetings of the Fellowship on both preaching and pastoring. He was made a Trustee of the Fellowship and in 1999 was accorded Honorary Life Membership.

He believed strongly that once a minister retired from his charge he should withdraw completely and let his successor get on with his own ministry. He practiced what he preached and such was the relationship with his successor in Hill Street, Drew Moore, that it was a pleasure for him to be invited back to Hill Street on special occasions. Until prevented by ill health, he returned to preach on at least one Sunday every Summer. On such occasions he would remark to the congregation "It's lovely to see the old faces I used to shake hands with".

In the autumn of 1993 he indicated that he felt the time had come for him to lay down his responsibilities in Greenwell Street. He preached his final sermon there on 19th December on Matthew 1:23 "Immanuel, God with us" and applied it in this way: God with us in childhood, youth, middle years and old age. Calling on people to put their trust in the Saviour he invited them to ask for his booklet "Salvation How?" Quite a number were taken. During the eight years he had worked in the congregation several people had come to faith, some were restored while many were encouraged and strengthened through his ministry. Right up to his death he continued to pray for and enquire about different people in the congregation he had come to love.

While no longer on the ministry team, he and Mary continued in membership and regularly attended the Sunday services and the midweek meeting for prayer and Bible study. He was still available for services and was approached by the Convener of the prolonged vacancy in Cloughey and Portavogie to take the services there for a number of Sundays to give some stability to the congregations. He expressed a burden for the Ards peninsula and his readiness to be used in that situation. His ministry of encouragement and challenge over those weeks was to make a vital contribution to those congregations.

Because of a series of inexplicable fainting attacks, which were becoming more frequent and more severe, he began to limit the number of preaching engagements he would undertake. Mary sought to caution him about this. Once when the phone rang she gave him a knowing and warning look as he went to the phone. A few moments later he returned with a wide grin on his face. Mary looked at him in disbelief. "John, you didn't say 'yes' to an invitation?".

"No", he replied, "but it was nice to know that at 83 I was invited to speak at a Youth Rally". It really warmed his heart.

On Sunday 3rd October 1999 he conducted the morning Harvest Thanksgiving service in First Donaghadee Presbyterian Church. At the time he was not to know it, but that was to be the last time he would preach.

On the 28th October he was admitted to the Ulster Hospital where he spent the next seven weeks. While there he was diagnosed with lung cancer but even then did not lose his zeal for the Lord. He often spoke to other patients and members of the nursing staff and had the privilege of seeing a fellow patient come to the Saviour through his witness.

On one occasion he was visited by the Moderator of the General Assembly. Before leaving, he read the Scriptures with John but just as he was about to pray John stopped him. Calling out to the other men in the ward, he told them "This is the Moderator and he's going to pray for all of us". Without a murmur books and newspapers were put down and the television set turned off while the Moderator prayed for John and his fellow patients.

Members of the hospital staff held him in the highest regard. A nurse going on a week's leave came to say 'goodbye' before going off duty. She told him that his attitude had made a real impact on the staff. His comment was "Praise the Lord for that".

During that spell in hospital he kept a diary. It is interspersed with appreciation for all the love and support from Mary and his family, for his many visitors and the dedication of the hospital staff. However, overwhelmingly it is full of expressions of praise and thanksgiving to the Lord for all His dealings with him through what were difficult and traumatic days.

At home he was lovingly cared for by Mary but he was becoming increasingly weak. As he was unable to attend Church, Mary had to give an account of everything that took place, including an update on who was present, and how different people were faring. Even in his weakness there was composure, humour and loving thoughtfulness. The last visit he made was to call with a man in hospital for whom he had been praying for years. Even though extremely weak himself, John expressed a concern that Mary should drive him to see his friend. He longed to see him coming to faith in Jesus Christ and felt it would be his last opportunity to speak to him about the Lord, and it was.

As his condition worsened during the summer of 2002 his prayers intensified that he wouldn't suffer more than he could bear, that he wouldn't linger and cause Mary and others to be burdened, that he wouldn't get confused and that he would die at home. He firmly believed in the sovereignty of God and was ready for whatever the Lord had for him. He frequently alluded to Psalm 31 v 15 'my times are in thy hand' as an expression of that trust and confidence. On every count the Lord graciously gave him his wish. Throughout all his illness, and especially during his last days, even though often in considerable discomfort, he showed remarkable resilience and continually thanked God for all His goodness to him. Psalm 146 v 2 was particularly precious to him 'While I live will I praise the Lord; I will sing praises unto my God while I have any being'.

Having fought a good fight, having kept the faith, having finished his course, he died at 7:15 am on Wednesday 21st August 2002.

John's Funeral Service took place in Greenwell Street Presbyterian Church on Friday 23rd August. One of the hymns he had chosen was a favourite of his and appropriately summed up his testimony

Loved with everlasting love,
Led by grace that love to know;
Spirit, breathing from above,
Thou hast taught me it is so.
O this full and perfect peace!
O this transport all divine!
In a love which cannot cease
I am His, and He is mine.

Heaven above is softer blue,
Earth around is sweeter green;
Something lives in every hue,
Christless eyes have never seen:
Birds with gladder songs o'erflow,
Flowers with deeper beauties shine,
Since I know, as now I know,
I am His, and He is mine.

His for ever, only His:
Who the Lord and me shall part?
Ah, with what a rest of bliss
Christ can fill the loving heart!
Heaven and earth may fade and flee,
First-born light in gloom decline;
But, while God and I shall be,
I am His, and He is mine.

(George Wade Robinson)

After the service his mortal remains were interred in Clandeboye Cemetery, Bangor.

9

ASSESSMENT

Although John was used of God in many different roles, he saw himself primarily and essentially as a parish minister.

He was meticulous in his preparation for preaching. Unless there was good reason otherwise, he would spend the mornings in his study and didn't appreciate being interrupted. Although he would read as widely as he could, it was the careful study of the Scriptures which took precedence over everything else. He was driven by a concern that he would himself understand God's Word so that he might be equipped to enable others to understand it. Painstakingly he typed his sermons word for word using the red ribbon to highlight important headings and then underlined in ink what he wanted to emphasize. However, in preaching he rarely consulted his script.

While minister in Bethany, one Sunday he suddenly discovered in the pulpit that he had no script with him. His assistant, George Cunningham, was leading the service and

John went back to the Minister's Room to pick up the script. However, it wasn't there. He went out to his car in Agnes Street, but it wasn't there either. Returning to the pulpit he hurriedly tried to jot down a few notes. He preached as he usually did and no one in the congregation was any wiser as to what had happened.

His sermons were marked by the authority of the Word of God and he preached as he lived, under the authority of that Word. He would agree with John Owen who wrote 'a man preacheth that sermon only well unto others, which preacheth itself in his own soul'.[1] One example of that is his approach to money. John was very particular about tithing as a Biblical principle and it was something he could get angry about, especially if he thought some Christian was cutting corners or cheating. For him the Bible was not a book to provide him with sermon material but The Guide for every aspect of his life.

In his preaching he used plain and simple language and he spoke with a voice that was clear and distinct. He never preached above the heads of the congregation. If anything annoyed him it would have been, as he saw it, any failure on his part to make the message of the gospel clear enough for any person to grasp. Of course, any blessing for any soul as the result of his preaching would be attributed by him unquestionably to the work of the Holy Spirit and not to any ability he might have.

Dr George Campbell Morgan was twice minister of Westminster Chapel, London. The three essentials of a sermon, he said, were 'truth, clarity and passion'. [2] All were present in John's preaching but his passion did not arise from some personality trait nor some induced emotion, but as a result of the Holy Spirit at work in his life.

He preached with sincerity and his burden for the souls of people was apparent as he pressed home the claims of the Lord Jesus on the lives of his hearers. He did so because he was thoroughly convinced of the importance of the Gospel. In his Minister's Letter to Hill Street Congregation in 1976 he wrote 'The Gospel of Jesus Christ is a spiritual necessity, not a far-fetched fairy story. You can dispense with much that seems essential to life, but not with the Gospel... the good news of the gospel brings reconciliation and life'. For him the Gospel was paramount and, while he admitted that he could as much as anyone else feel distressed by social problems, he believed intensely in the need for personal conversion. The last time he spoke at a meeting of the Westminster Fellowship he quoted with strong approval words of Thomas Hugh Keir 'We are sent not to preach sociology but salvation, not economics but evangelism, not the new social order but the new birth, not a reorganization but a new creation, not democracy but the gospel, not civilization but Christ. We are ambassadors, not diplomats'.

It was no exaggeration when William Caughey, then Clerk of Session in Strean Presbyterian Church, called him, 'The prince of preachers'.

Robert L Dabney wrote 'To speak for God to men is a sacred and responsible task. To speak for men to God is not less responsible and is more solemn'.[3] John was a man who did both with conviction. That conviction is well expressed by Richard Baxter ' Our whole work must be carried on in a sense of our insufficiency and in a pious believing dependence on Christ. We must go to Him for light and life and strength, who sends us on our work...Prayer must carry on our work as well as preaching: he preacheth not heartily to his people, that will not pray for them. If we prevail not with God to give them faith and repentance, we are unlikely to prevail with them to believe and repent.' [4]

From the time of his conversion prayer was a vital part of his life. He was disciplined in this as in so much else and refused to let anything divert him either in the morning or at night. He would say "You can go to work without your corn flakes and toast but not without speaking to the Lord". No matter how long and busy the day would have been he would get down on his knees beside his bed and talk to the Lord about his work, thanking Him for the help given and invariably praying for the salvation of people had visited. Mary recalls one night when they arrived home very late and very tired. She suggested they go straight to bed, saying that the Lord understood and knew they were grateful for the help given that day. She felt rebuked when he replied, "That being so, it would only take a few minutes to express our gratitude" and then he knelt down and prayed.

Not only was he a man of prayer himself but he was convinced of the importance of prayer in the life of any church. He constantly reminded his congregations of the necessity for prayer, as William Still put it, 'no church can live without prayer'.[5] John's thoughts on the issue are expressed in this extract from his letter to Hill Street in 1980. 'There is no worthwhile gain in any work of God without the agony of earnest, believing prayer, and the first steps in going forward must be in that direction. It is from a praying people that effectiveness in evangelizing, teaching, visiting and witnessing stems. Without the power of the Holy Spirit, given in answer to prayer, there will be no life-giving virtue in any of our activities, though they be multiplied a thousand times'.

In this respect Jonathan Edwards' comments about David Brainerd, missionary to the American Indians, are relevant also to John. "His history shows us the right way to success in the work of the ministry...Animated with love to Christ and the souls of men, how did he 'labour always fervently', not only in word and doctrine, in public and private, but in prayers day and night, 'wrestling with God' in secret, and 'travailing in birth', with unutterable groans and agonies, 'until Christ were formed' in the hearts of the people to whom he was sent". [6]

John too was motivated by a twofold love- a love for Jesus and a love for the souls of people of all ages. He was a deeply spiritual man. He loved the Saviour and sought to live close to Him, serving Him as best he knew how. At the same time he was 'down to earth' , aware that he lived and served in this world. However, like Abraham , he looked 'forward to the city with foundations, whose architect and builder is God' (Heb 11:10).

He was burdened for the souls of people and he loved to be with people. Always interested in individuals, he possessed an amazing capacity to remember names. Even in his retirement he would ask about certain folk whom he recalled from his days in the Belfast City Mission. He showed great compassion for people and was ready to bring not only spiritual help but practical assistance if it was within his ability and power.

If one aspect of his character stands out it is his forthrightness. When someone said or did something he didn't agree with, he had no hesitation in letting them know his mind. He had a habit of looking at you from under his brows which indicated you had incurred his extreme displeasure. Such straightforwardness didn't come from a spirit of vindictiveness or controversy for the sake of it. Rather, his plain speaking arose from strongly held convictions which were determined by his obedience to the Scriptures.

John had a great rapport with friends and colleagues and he would often make witty remarks, often at their expense, though always in the best of taste. However, there were things that he would not joke about and on occasions he would chide colleagues if he felt they were overstepping the line in this regard. On one occasion, at a meal, one of his close friends made a derogatory remark about what he regarded as 'useless ministers'. He was immediately chided by John for speaking ill of brother ministers. Some around the table thought that he was jesting too, but he was being serious and he made it clear that a line had been crossed which ought not to have been.

Many a person has remarked that when they first met John, especially in his younger years with his dark hair and eyebrows, they were somewhat put off. He gave the impression of someone who was quite grim and severe or at the very least somewhat 'dour'. But then you would see that infectious smile which belied such an impression and no-one would be long in his company before they discovered a man who had a warm and caring personality.

That was very evident in his pastoral ministry, especially in the visitation of homes. John was thoroughly convinced that it was an essential aspect of parish ministry for the minister to be regularly in the homes of the people and to be available to them, particularly in times of need. In fact he was quite adamant about this and argued that you had to win the right to challenge people with the gospel. Whenever he could he sought to bring conversations round to spiritual matters and often would ask "what ails you at Jesus?". Many bear testimony to the fact that, as he met with people in their homes and shared with them in their varied and different experiences, they knew him to be a man who was deeply concerned for their spiritual welfare.

John had a great gift of getting alongside people whatever their circumstances and this was true of his hospital visitation. He would greet the patient with a broad smile and would shake them warmly by the hand and then sit close to them and engage them in conversation at a level with which they could cope. Sometimes, if circumstances favoured it, he would read a short portion of Scripture, though often he would just pray with the person. He would pray for the individual, giving thanks to God for the person and other matters related to them and their needs; but he would also preach in his prayer, for all the elements of the gospel would be there and in a praying posture he would have as much attention as the person was able to give as, in prayer, he commended the Saviour to them and they to the Saviour. Many a life would benefit from ministers who would employ that pattern in their visitation.

He exuded an air of determination. That was evident from the manner in which he rode his bicycle as a young man, for he would crouch down over the handlebars and fix his gaze ahead of him and would not be distracted from reaching his goal. It was seen in his student years when he was determined to fulfil the requirements to enter the ministry. In fulfilling that ministry he was determined to preach the gospel in truth and clarity and to live faithfully for his Lord and Saviour, whatever others might think of him.

Already note has been taken of evidence of his wise counsel, capacity for hard work, strength of character, tact, kindness and integrity. He was an example to any minister whose desire was to be faithful to his ordination vows. Nevertheless, he would be the first to admit that he had his own limitations and would acknowledge that any 'success' in his life and ministry could only be attributed to the work of the Holy Spirit.

A sense of humour and love of fun were integral parts of his character. A book could easily be filled with accounts of that and some we have already recorded. He could use that tactfully when things were not as he would like them to be. On an aeroplane going on holiday to Tunisia, along with other passengers he was annoyed at the antics of a young boy who seemed to be beyond the control of his mother. Eventually John spoke to her, "Missus, would your wee fellow not like to play outside for a while?"

On one occasion during a meeting in Hill Street a member was insisting that a particular thing could be done. John, on the other hand was insisting it couldn't be done for in his estimation it was impossible. The member said " Mr. Girvan, nothing is impossible." John took off his glasses, laid them on the table, looked at him and calling him by name said " Mr. X, did you ever try striking a match on a bar of soap?"

Essentially a humble man, he never forget his roots. Nor did he seek the limelight. Like many other holders of that office, one aspect of being Moderator he dreaded was being in the forefront of attention, especially from the media. However, he was willing to stand up for himself, when necessary. In a BBC television interview just after his nomination, Sean Rafferty mentioned a particular issue and something John was reported to have said. "Now, Now", said John and then proceeded to put the record straight. Incidentally, he was highly regarded in the media, which certainly did not always agree with what he had to say, but respected him for his integrity and conviction.

While he appreciated order and decorum, he did not like pomposity and show. Indeed he went so far as to quickly deflate any temptation to egotism even in his friends. Although he had given much encouragement to a young minister in his studies, when he subsequently gained a Ph.D., John remarked to him with a shrug of his shoulders and the twinkle of a smile: "Nothing great in that. It only stands for paper-hanger and decorator!" When he himself was awarded a Doctor of Divinity degree on becoming Moderator, he had to stand some banter from others but he enjoyed every bit of it. One member of the Armagh Presbytery on congratulating him noted that the Presbytery now boasted of no less than five doctors including Girvan but added, "And if you had a headache there's not one of them could give you an Aspirin!"

He never lost his sense of gratitude to God for his own salvation and for his calling to preach. Frequently he would express it in these terms: "When I get to glory I want to say 'thank you' to my Saviour first of all for saving me and then for giving me the privilege of, however feebly, preaching his Gospel".

Only those close to John knew of how sensiti\
was. Converts who did not go on with the Lord d
him. He was grieved when he discovered professin
not living up to standards of honesty and integrity. He felt hurts
deeply. There were occasions when he was misunderstood.
There were people he thought he could depend upon who let
him down. He faced verbal attacks for his strongly held
convictions. He endured abusive letters in correspondence
columns. Yet he would not retaliate in kind, nor did he hold
grudges and would pray tenderly for those with whom he
differed.

On one occasion he was attacked in an unfair and vicious
manner in the local newspaper by a minister of another
denomination. Although urged by some of his elders and other
friends to reply, he chose to let the matter rest. Another friend
entered into correspondence in the paper and eventually his
attacker, who was well outpointed, dropped the matter.
Interestingly, some years later John received an apology from
the offending minister.

John was able to adopt such an attitude because he
confidently left all such matters and people to a higher Judge
than he. Indeed, he would take that approach over many issues.
When some matter had to be dealt with he would say "We've
sought the Lord about it and discussed it. We've done what we
feel is right. We're not going to worry about it. Let's leave it all
now to the Lord; it's His responsibility". His simple
uncomplicated faith and trust in God's power and faithfulness
meant that a sleepless night over some issue was a rarity in his
experience.

He was very human. He didn't like to be disturbed,
especially if he were watching wrestling or more especially a
football match on TV and someone phoned or called. On one
occasion he was engrossed in a very exciting World Cup match

when a stranger called. Mary brought him in and John immediately asked, "Do you like football?" When the man replied in the negative, John told him " Well, sit there until this match is over and I'll talk to you then." So he did.

He didn't always appreciate criticism about his driving, which he thought was impeccable. He could be impatient when things didn't move as quickly as he would like. Devoting himself with such commitment to the Lord's work, he lived by the principle which he frequently quoted: "It's better to burn out than rust out".

John had a high opinion of the work of the ministry which he once summarized as 'consecration towards God and commitment towards people'. He affirmed throughout his own ministry the requirements set out in the first question asked of an ordinand, "So far as you know your own heart have you been induced to seek the office of the ministry from love to God and from a sincere desire to win souls to Christ and to promote the Divine glory?". What is very clear from any reading of his addresses to ministers and his charges to those newly ordained is his conviction that no higher honour could be conferred on any man. Therefore it was something of a disappointment to him when he encountered those who did not share his profound sense of responsibility or his convictions concerning the ministry.

John and Mary enjoyed a very special and happy marriage, which they viewed as a partnership in the Lord's work. It was often a source of concern to Mary that he rarely took time off on a regular basis. Nevertheless, John constantly displayed an air of relaxed calmness. When he did go on holiday he would take with him a supply of books, usually novels and especially detective stories. He would listen frequently to Country and Western and Gospel music and of course sport was always at the forefront of his interests.

John had a strong clear tenor voice and loved to sing. He was also gifted musically and played the electric guitar, flute, tin whistle and harmonica. Many a gathering was enlivened as a result. But he also used his gifts in the cause of the gospel. Once he visited a man who was quite apathetic to the message of the gospel. Noticing a fiddle on the wall John asked him if he played it. Given an affirmative answer John excused himself and left the house. A short time later he returned with his flute and the two of them played for hours. A barrier was broken down and the man listened intently to what John had to say about salvation.

It was not in the providence of God that John would have any children of his own but he had a deep love for every child he met. He was so much at home with them and was at his ease playing with them in their homes and they thought the world of him.

However, no-one but the Lord knows the number of his spiritual children. On a purely human level so many owe John their lives for he was the instrument in the hands of God to lead many to know the Saviour. Some of them he knew about and it always delighted him to hear of those who had come to faith through his ministry but there are so many more he never met whose lives the Lord transformed through the life and words of his servant. Some had come to faith through the regular preaching in his congregations and through personal contacts at home or in hospital. Many came to faith through the missions he conducted throughout Ireland in various Halls and Churches. John was very much a Presbyterian by conviction and while he spoke at meetings in different denominations the Presbyterian Church in Ireland was his first love. Over a period of some 34 years he preached at missions in over 80 congregations of the Presbyterian Church. William Craig's assessment at his farewell reception in Hill Street that John was "the man through whom more people in Northern Ireland have been brought to Christ than any other living person" was truly justified.

There are many who will praise the day the Lord brought John Girvan into contact with them. But he would quite readily identify with the words of Mrs. A R Cousins whose hymn was based on the letters of Samuel Rutherford who had to endure exile in Aberdeen from his congregation in Anwoth on the Solway Firth.

> *"Oh! if one soul from Anwoth*
> *Meet me at God's right hand,*
> *My heaven will be two heavens*
> *In Immanuel's land"*

William Booth, the founder of the Salvation Army was once asked what was the secret of his success. He replied, "God has had all there was of me to have". Unquestionably, the same could be be said of John. He was totally and unreservedly committed to the Lord and in His hands proved to be a faithful servant.

Especially in his later years John spoke with some emotion of those he had known who had once been strong in their faith, members of the Evangelical Union, fellow students, colleagues in the ministry, who had been so keen for the Lord but who over the years had lost their evangelical zeal or their enthusiasm for the Word of God or had drifted from their commitment to Christ. "I know of nothing", said C H Spurgeon, "which I would choose to have, as the subject of my ambition for life, than to be kept faithful to my God to death, still to be a soul-winner, still to be a true herald of the cross, and testify the name of Jesus to the last hour". [7] That was an ambition shared by John and it was fulfilled. His whole life as a Christian and as a Minister of the Gospel was marked by consistent faithfulness to the Lord, to the

Word of God and to the Church of Christ. He held Biblically based convictions tenaciously to the end of his life. He adhered to Biblical standards which guided his behaviour, attitudes and actions from the time of his conversion. What he was at the end of his ministerial activity he had been throughout all his years of service in the Presbyterian Church in Ireland since his time with the Belfast City Mission. 'Sure and Steadfast', the motto of the Boys'Brigade was truly exemplified in his life.

There is perhaps no better summary of John Girvan than in the words of John 10:41-42 : 'John did no miracle: but all things that John spoke of this man (Jesus) were true. And many believed on Him there'.

1. 'The Works of John Owen', Banner of Truth, Edinburgh, 1995, Vol 16 p 76

2. G C Morgan, 'Preaching', Baker Book House, Grand Rapids,1937 (1974 reprint), p 14f

3. R L Dabney, 'Evangelical Eloquence: A Course of Lectures on Preaching', Banner of Truth Trust, Edinburgh,1999, p 347

4. R Baxter, 'The Reformed Pastor', SCM Press, London, 1963, p 77f

5. 'Letters of William Still', Banner of Truth Trust, Edinburgh, 1984, p 30

6. Jonathan Edwards, "The Life of Rev David Brainerd", Baker Book House, Grand Rapids, 1978, p 356.

7. Metropolitan Tabernacle Pulpit, Vol 10 (1864) reprinted by Pilgrim Publications, Pasadena Texas 1991 p. 87

APPENDIX A

SALVATION HOW?

The Bible makes it clear that God is both able and willing to save every man and woman from the guilt, the penalty and the power of sin. Think, for example, of verses like Hebrews 7 v 25, "Therefore He is able to save completely those who come to God through Him, because He always lives to intercede for them." 2 Peter 3 v 9, "The Lord is not slow in keeping His promise, as some understand slowness. He is patient with you not wanting anyone to perish, but everyone to come to repentance." These references show both the ability and the willingness of God to save. There may be, however, a question in our minds regarding exactly how we come into the experience of personal salvation. I am thinking of three words which describe the stages through which the enquirer passes as he comes into possession of eternal life. The first word is:-

1. AWARENESS

Before you can know the experience of salvation you must become aware of need. You won't be bothered to consult a doctor unless you are aware that there is something wrong with your physical condition. Neither will you be very interested in the matter of salvation unless you are conscious of your need of it. Most people will admit that they are not all they ought to be, but unless their unworthiness begins to trouble them they will never be moved to do anything about it. This is the work of the Holy Spirit, it is sometimes called "conviction of sin".

At any rate, the person concerned begins to see as probably never before, that there is something wrong within him, and he experiences a sense of uneasiness that cannot be removed. This occurs to a greater or lesser degree in different people, but the thing that matters is that the person becomes aware that all is not well.

But having realised that all is not well, and having a desire to have things made right, what then? The second word I am thinking of is:-

2. ACKNOWLEDGEMENT

Not just acknowledgement that there is uneasiness, but;

(a) Acknowledgement of the sin that has caused the uneasiness.

The Bible is emphatic in stating that man's basic trouble is his sin. Isaiah 59 v 2 "But your iniquities have separated you from your God; your sins have hidden His face from you, so that He will not hear." Jeremiah 17 v 9, "The heart is deceitful above all things and beyond cure. Who can understand it?" Romans 3 v 23, "All have sinned and fall short of the glory of God." The Scriptures show that man is a sinner and that it is his sin which makes him unhappy when the Holy Spirit begins to deal with him.

(b) There must also be acknowledgement that God punishes sin.

Romans 6 v 23, "The wages of sin is death." James 1 v 15, "Sin, when it is full-grown, gives birth to death." Ezekiel 18 v 4, "The soul who sins is the one who will die." It would be out of harmony with the nature of God if He were to treat sin as if it didn't matter. His attitude to sin has always been the same, it is an attitude of judgement. So then, the judgement of God rests upon sin and upon the one who commits it.

(c) Then there must be an acknowledgement of the work of Christ.

John 3 v 16, "For God so loved the world that He gave His one and only Son, that whoever believes in Him shall not perish but have everlasting life." It was never the will of God to inflict pain or suffering on anyone, but He could not permit the sin of man to go unjudged or unpunished. Sin must be punished either in the person who commits it, or in someone else. But that someone else must be one who himself had never committed sin, and the only person in that category was the Son of God.

And so, Jesus Christ came into the world. He lived a spotlessly pure life- Acts 10 v 38, "He went around doing good." John 7 v 46, "No one ever spoke the way this Man does." John 19 v 6, " Pilate said, I find no basis for a charge against Him." - and at the end of such a life, Jesus died on the Cross for the sin of the world. Isaiah 53 vv 5,6, "He was pierced for our transgressions, He was crushed for our iniquities, the punishment that brought us peace was upon Him, and by His wounds we are healed. We all, like sheep have gone astray; each of us has turned to his own way; and the Lord has laid on Him the iniquity of us all." Ist Peter 3 v 18, "For Christ died for sins once for all, the righteous for the unrighteous, to bring you to God."

There it is then, our sin is real, we are aware of it. That sin must be punished, and the punishment is death, separation from God. But Jesus Christ, in Whom there was no sin, has taken the punishment instead of the sinner, and so the sinner may go free. That briefly, is God's plan of salvation. The next question is, how does this salvation become mine? The third word I have in mind is:-

3. ACCEPTANCE

In accepting Jesus Christ as my Saviour, and His work on the Cross as done on my behalf, there are one or two things that must be noted. I cannot save myself, only God can do that, but there are certain factors on my side that cannot be ignored. One of these factors is:-

(a) Repentance

Luke 13 v 5, "But unless you repent, you too will all perish." The Shorter Catechism gives an excellent definition of repentance, it is "a saving grace, whereby a sinner, out of a true sense of his sin and apprehension of the mercy of God in Christ, doth with grief and hatred of his sin, turn from it unto God, with full purpose of and endeavour after new obedience." That is to say, there must be both sorrow for sin and willingness to turn from it. There is no point in saying that I want to be saved from my sin, if in fact, I am not willing to have done with it.

Now to be willing to leave my sin does not mean that I am able to break with it. I may have formed certain sinful habits which hold me in their power, but before I can be saved, I must be willing to be released from them. Where there is willingness God will supply the ability. So then, one important factor in accepting Christ is repentance. Another is:-

(b) Faith

The Shorter Catechism defines faith in Jesus Christ as "a

saving grace, whereby we receive and rest upon Him alone for salvation, as He is offered to us in the Gospel." Faith is simply belief, but it is belief in action. I may believe in the ability of the doctor to deal with a particular complaint. I go to him and listen to all he has to say. He gives me a prescription which he says will cure me. I believe with all my heart that what he says is true. But unless I put my belief into action, go to the chemist, receive the prescribed remedy, and take it, I shall not be cured. To go to the doctor, and to take the advice and medicine he prescribes-that is real faith.

I may believe I need to be saved, I may believe that I am a sinner and that my sin must be punished. I may believe that Jesus Christ has taken the punishment that was my due and that I may go free- I may believe all that and yet not be saved. My belief must express itself in action. What kind of action? The act of receiving into my heart and life Jesus Christ as my Saviour and Lord. John 1 v 12, "Yet to all who received Him, to those who believed in His name, He gave the right to become children of God." Salvation has been provided in a Person, that Person is Jesus Christ, and to receive salvation is to receive Jesus Christ.

How do I receive Jesus Christ? This is the question that often presents the greatest difficulty. Revelation 3 v 20, "Here I am. I stand at the door and knock. If anyone hears my voice and opens the door, I will come in." The speaker is Jesus Christ. The door He refers to is the life of the individual. He states that He is knocking. The awareness of my need being brought home to me is in fact, Christ knocking by the Holy Spirit. This uneasiness I feel, this sense of not being right with God is Christ knocking at my life. Now He declares that if I hear Him knocking- if I am aware of my need, and open the door; that is, if I am willing to put my faith in Him, if I am willing to invite Him into my life, He will come in. And so, to exercise faith in Jesus Christ is simply to ask Him to come into my life and believe that He comes in.

Will I feel that He has come in? There is nothing mentioned about feelings, it is a matter of taking God at His word- He says He will come in if I ask Him; I ask Him, and I believe He keeps His promise. There then, are two necessary elements in accepting Jesus Christ as Saviour. First, I repent of my sin- I am willing to turn from all that I know to be displeasing to Him. Second, I ask Him to come into my heart and life, and asking Him, I believe He comes in-that is faith. There is one other thing worth remembering, it is:-

(c) Witnessing for Christ

Romans 10 v 9, "If you shall confess with your mouth, 'Jesus is Lord', and believe in your heart that God raised Him from the dead, you will be saved." We must be willing to bear witness to the fact that Jesus has become our Saviour. Matthew 10 v 32, "Whoever acknowledges Me before men, I will also acknowledge him before My Father in Heaven." Confession of Jesus Christ as Saviour is honouring to Him, and as well as that, it lets other people know exactly where we stand, and they know what to expect from us.

How is this new life which we receive when Jesus Christ becomes our Saviour to be maintained?

Physical life must have food. Spiritual life must also be fed and nourished. Jesus said, "Man does not live on bread alone, but on every word that comes from the mouth of God." We must read the Bible every day, God feeds the new life in this way. We must also pray. God talks to us through His Word; He wants us to talk to Him through prayer. To neglect either of these means of grace is to imperil our walk and witness as His children. Then too, we should cultivate helpful relationships. We must not shut ourselves away from those who are not Christians, but the fellowship of people who are like-minded is of very great value.

Are you ready to receive Jesus Christ as Saviour and Lord? Make this your prayer.

"Lord, I know I am a sinner, and that my sin must be punished. I know also that my sin has been punished in Jesus Christ. I repent of my sin, and with Your help, will turn from it. I accept Jesus Christ as my Saviour now. Help me to go forth and witness by lip and life that I am His, and He is mine. Amen."

APPENDIX B

NOTES OF A SERMON ON MATTHEW 18:3

One of India's great men Scrinavas Shastri said to Dr Stanley Jones, "I'm not religious, but I'm not irreligious. Religion is just not real to me. I wish it were. How did your religion become real to you?" Dr Jones gave the man his testimony and he replied, "I see what I need, it is conversion".

In our text Jesus makes one of those sweeping statements of His. Yes, He is talking to the disciples, but the use of that word 'whosoever' indicates that what He is saying has a far wider application than the little circle around Him. The basic conditions that drew from our Lord the words of our text have not really changed, and the need of conversion today is as real as it has ever been.

You remember what Jesus said about the unclean spirit being driven out of a house. He said it was left empty, swept and garnished. And that is the situation in which modern man finds himself whatever the colour of his skin and whatever his education or culture. Modern man's soul has been swept of many a superstition, it has been furnished with many pieces of scientific knowledge and with many scientific conveniences, but it is still empty of any real way of life. Man is filled with mental confusion and spiritual chaos, he seems to know nothing of the life that is really positive-he needs conversion.

And yet it is a fact that many people today are quite ready to dispute the need for any such thing as a thorough going conversion. Oh they will admit to a sense of boredom, frustration, meaninglessness and loneliness and maybe we as preachers are too ready to meet people on those grounds and talk about the need for Jesus as a Friend for the lonely or about the sense of purpose Jesus can give to the frustrated. Like the doctor who listens to the patient's description of his illness and then proceeds to treat accordingly instead of thoroughly examining the man and making an independent diagnosis, an approach that is tantamount to allowing the patient to be his own doctor. The real problem is not friendlessness, loneliness, boredom or frustration, it is deeper than that.

One of the wonderful things about New Testament days is that there were many who were asking the right kind of questions. One asked "What shall I do that I may have eternal life?" After Peter's sermon on the day of Pentecost, the people asked " Men and brethren, what shall we do?" The Philippian jailer asked "What must I do to be saved?"

Dr Chandu Ray, Bishop of Karachi, visited a college in Pakistan where most of the students were Muslims. He offered personal interviews and over 100 accepted. Dr Ray said that they did not want to discuss his attitude to Islam or Christianity or even theology. Their great question was "Is there any way of release from the soiled conscience which torments us?"

And I want to say right away that if you are not a born again person, whatever other needs you may have, the need for conversion is the greatest.

One thing so noticeable about the preaching of the Lord Jesus was the fact that He went straight to the point. He was provokingly personal, people knew He was talking to them-His attitude to Nicodemus was typical - "Ye must be born again".

What kind of people have we got in the congregation this evening?

1. **There are those to whom their religion is real.** To them forgiveness is real, the feeling of guilt has been removed. There is a sense of being at one with God. Life has a meaning it never had. Jesus is more than a historical character-they can talk about Him as a personal Saviour, they have come to see that His life on earth and His death

had a personal application for them. They can say with the Apostle "He loved me and gave Himself for me".

And this has a direct effect on all their relationships. Their attitude to their very work is transformed. What they now do is as unto the Lord. Prayer has taken on a new meaning, the Bible is a new Book and at least a little of the experience of Paul is theirs- "To me to live is Christ". Oh, like the blind man who received his sight, they haven't all the answers, but they know that something happened and they can never be the same again. Is that you?

2.   **Then there are those to whom religion is unreal.** Oh yes, they believe in God all right, they love their Church and help in every good work. They have no intention of playing the hypocrite. But somehow the whole thing is so outward and so dissatisfying and formal. It has not got the satisfying ingredients the preacher and the Word of God say it should. We go through the mechanics of worship but there is just not the living vital note about it all there ought to be. What about daily life, job, career, and the future?

If we knew we were to be called away to-night, we are not sure that all is well. There are crowds of people in all our Churches just like that, it may be there are some like that here. Nicodemus was in that category, so was the rich young ruler.

3.   **There are those to whom religion is nothing.** They probably believe in having some sort of connection with the Church, if they were to be married the wedding would have to be in the Church and the minister would certainly be called in in the case of a death. But it ends there. They might even go along to Church or a special mission to please a friend, but the whole thing is completely empty, and the fact doesn't bother them very much.

I cannot tell to which of these three groups you belong, but if it is to either of the latter two, your greatest need is the theme of this service. You need to be converted.

Alexander Pope, the writer, was heard to pray, "Lord. make me a better man". One of his servants heard it and couldn't help saying, "It would be easier to make you a new man." And that is exactly what it means to be converted. If any man be in Christ he is a new creature.

There are three elements in Conversion that are suggested by our text

1. **Except ye be converted - A new direction.** The word means 'to turn'. You see, we are all going in the wrong direction. "All we like sheep have gone astray". Paul to the Romans "There is none that seeketh after God, there is none that doeth good, they are all gone out of the way".

    The very first step in getting right with God is recognition of one's wrongness in the sight of God; you will never seek a new direction unless you are aware that you are going in the wrong direction.

    There are two sides to this matter of getting right with God-the Godward and the manward sides. It is God who carries out the work of the New Birth but there must be the willingness on the part of man to have the New Birth, and this is what conversion really is. You remember Jesus said "Come unto Me and I will give you rest". He gives rest, but we must come.

    The decision 'to turn' is something that no one in this world can make for you! It is great to see people brought to the place of decision-but at that place you will stand alone-not even God can make you say 'Yes' - it is your decision. I think of Rebekah and Isaac, and of the rich young ruler, and Pilate.

    The word conversion comes from two Latin words

'vertare'= 'to turn' and 'con' = 'with'. the decision to turn is yours, but thank God, He is able to help us to put the decision into practice. If we turn in the sense that is meant here, we turn with God. Once this decision is made, the putting it into effect is easy because God is with us, we turn with Him.

A new direction! Don't some of us need to begin going in a new direction? It will certainly mean a break with the old life, maybe not easy, but because God is there, it is not impossible.

2.   **And become like little children- a new life.** Of course, only God can effect this. We can't really make ourselves little children, we can't really begin all over again.

But this is what Jesus was getting at when He talked with Nicodemus- "Ye must be born from above". It is the work of God. And just as you entered the world of physical material things through physical birth, so there can be no membership of that spiritual world except through the medium of spiritual birth.

New birth means new life and what a life it is! Not a new page in the history of your life, but a completely new book, with the old one tossed onto the heap of forgotten things. I always fear lest people get the impression that what we preach is merely a set of rules to be obeyed and thus we enter the Kingdom of God. What we preach is a life to be lived- a life with all the spiritual likes and dislikes, the inclinations and tendencies that follow from the experience of Regeneration or new birth. Yes, this is beginning all over again and it is beginning with God.

3.   **The Kingdom of God- a new Loyalty.** By conversion you become a member of a new kingdom. That doesn't mean that you are no longer in the world with all its sinful sordid

temptations. Jesus told the disciples that they are in the world and yet not of it. This life makes demands.

Hitherto we live to please ourselves-we followed the paths of decent, respectable living, but the desire to gratify self was always present.

The converted person has a new King. Previously self was on the throne of his life, now it is Jesus Christ and henceforth behaviour and conduct are controlled by His will. Jesus declared "I do always those things which please My Father in heaven" and the converted person is now in that category.

What is your reaction to all this? You are thinking that this is a difficult life and you are right, but the thing that really matters is this, it is no longer I who struggle along trying to overcome this habit or that. I am now possessed by a Stronger than I myself am. He has shown Himself too powerful for satan and sin, and by the Holy Spirit He is dwelling within this life so that what He wills, I will.

And that is just where the battle is lost or won. Am I willing to hand over this life to the control of the One who wants to save it and fill it with a new purpose and use it for His glory? May God help us to think the matter through and then do what we know to be the right thing.

APPENDIX C

TRANSCRIPT OF A SERMON ON 1 KINGS 17:1

The first eleven chapters of I Kings deal with the period of the reign of Solomon over Israel. He was the third king. There was Saul who turned out to be a real failure, followed by David who was declared to have been a man after God's own heart. He was followed by Solomon. When he came to the throne he was barely 20 years of age. But he had the benefit of his father David's counsel and example. In I Kings 2:2 David said 'I am about to die, be strong, show yourself a man and pay attention to what the Lord requires'. In 3:3 Solomon is stated to have shown his love for the Lord by walking according to the statutes of his father David 'except that he offered sacrifices and burnt incense on high places'. That word 'except' is mighty significant. Solomon's one major fault early in his reign was inconsistency in meeting the Mosaic requirements concerning places of legitimate worship. The high places referred to here were simply mounds of earth or stones upon which sacrifices were offered to false gods and they were dotted all over the land. But away far back as the Book of Leviticus in 17 v 3-5 God forbade the worship of Himself, Jehovah, in any of those situations. 'Except' may seem unimportant but is significant.

In 3:5-15 Solomon's prayer for wisdom in preference to wealth or power or even long life is most commendable. It shows that this young king already possessed a fair degree of wisdom for surely it was a mark of wisdom that he should ask for wisdom. There is one thing, however, that is worth noticing. He didn't ask for spiritual wisdom, that insight in holy things which is the fruit of close fellowship and communion with God. In 3: 12 we're told that in response to Solomon's request God said 'I will do what you have asked. I will give you wisdom and discernment in administering justice'. And in 4 v 29-34 we're told that God gave Solomon such wisdom that he excelled over all the leading philosophers of his day, either in Israel or beyond its borders. But, I repeat, there's no mention of spiritual wisdom and, as we read through the story of this man's life, we see that at crucial times that kind of wisdom was missing. The early years of Solomon's reign were marked by wise decisions, discriminating judgment, excellent wisdom, the growth of his empire, the splendour of his court and the building of the magnificent temple. The later years, however, were marred by the decline of the kingdom brought about by his extravagant luxuries, his notorious sensuality and his open apostasy from God. Ch 11: 4 tells us that he was led astray because his heart was not fully devoted to the Lord. Did it begin with compromise regarding the high places?

Are you a Christian, truly and genuinely born again? You can point to the time, to the day, to the date, to the place and all that. I want to ask you is your heart fully devoted to the Lord? Is your whole personality focussed upon serving Him? Is His Kingdom the rule of your life? Or is it your own little kingdom?

I am convinced that the dangers that face the very existence of the Church in our part of the world are not dangers from outside but dangers within the Church herself. As I read my newspapers and think of the state of things at home and overseas, the Church in general and her members in particular are not devoted to the Lord. The world attacks, it brings its pressures upon us and we compromise.

Note the outcome of lack of devotion. In 11:11 God says to Solomon 'I will take the kingdom from you and will give it to your servant'. It is often said that a full cup isn't easy to carry. How delightful to see a man or a woman who has committed his or her life to Christ in youth continue in that commitment to the very end. It rejoices my heart as I look back as far as my City

Mission days and think of lasses and lads who were in my Sunday School in those days, who came to the Lord, and to meet them nowadays and know that they are bright and shining for Jesus. Are you as keen for the Lord today as you were in the early days of your Christian experience? The answer to that question is easy to find for it gives rise to another question. Does God get first place in your reckoning or is the furtherance of your own personal interest the thing that is given priority? Are we guilty of compromise? Solomon did that which was right in the sight of the Lord. He followed in the steps of his father David, except...

After the death of Solomon the slide had commenced. Shakespeare wrote 'The evil that men do lives after them'. Solomon not only brought dishonour to God and the memory of his father but he sowed the seeds of disaster for the nation at large. After Solomon had gone the kingdom of Israel was split. The northern part consisting of 10 tribes continued to be called Israel and the southern part of two tribes was called Judah. For the next 86 years the northern kingdom had eight kings in succession and of every single one of them we read 'he did that which was evil in the eyes of the Lord'. All that is recorded in ch 12- 17 bring before us a story that is depressing in the extreme. Did it begin with Solomon's compromise? I hazard a guess that it did.

God had not forgotten and God had not lost interest. Chs 17-22 show that God had been preparing a man for the situation. Just as we read that 'when the fulness of the time was come, God sent forth his Son' so in this situation when the picture seemed blackest and darkest a shaft of light appeared. Those chapters are occupied with the ministry of one of the most remarkable men of the whole story of Israel, Elijah the prophet. Elijah came on the scene during the reign of Ahab king of northern kingdom of Israel and no greater tribute could be paid to any man than that which was given to Elijah by some of the Jews in the day of our Lord. As they listened to the mighty ministry of Jesus Christ they said 'This is Elijah'.

The state of things when Elijah came were such that the spiritual and moral condition of the nation was at an all time low. I Kings 16:30 says Ahab 'did more evil in the eyes of the Lord than any of those before him'. Note 'in the eyes of the Lord'. There were those who regarded the situation as quite acceptable. Things seemed to be prospering, everything was going nicely enough. But it needs to be remembered that material prosperity is not necessarily proof of the favour of God. The nation had taken on the culture and customs of the heathen around them. Idolatrous temples and heathen altars filled the land. We read that the people drank in iniquity like water and shameful sexual practices and rites were the order of the day. The fact was that the glory of the Lord had departed from Israel and thick spiritual darkness covered the land. The slide started with Solomon and his compromise. So wise in so many ways but so foolish in the area that mattered most. How simply and subtly it began. In Moses' day the people became restless and insisted on having a king. Moses became aware that there would come a time when they would insist in being like the nations around them and said in Deuteronomy 17 'the king that you appoint must not multiply wealth, wives or horses'. Solomon became guilty on all three counts. I Kings 11:6 says about him 'he did not follow the Lord completely'.

I wonder if we can identify with that kind of scenario. We can look back to a time when there was a genuine commitment of ourselves to Jesus Christ and we made up our minds that we would go through with God as I did the night I was converted. I remember saying 'Lord I don't understand this very well. I don't know what it's going to mean but so far as I know, Lord, it is all or nothing'. You can identify with that. Have we been true to that commitment and have we experienced the blessing of God accordingly? Or is it possible that as time went on standards became compromised, the pressure of the world around us became too great and we succumbed and the kingdom of God and His righteousness are no longer the dominant feature of our lives?

Into that situation there came a man. God is always looking for a person. Schemes and programmes have their place but God says 'I sought for a man'. We read of John the Baptist, 'There was a man sent from God'. If ever there was a man sent from God for a particular crisis in the Old Testament it was this man Elijah. The last 6 chapters of I Kings contain the most exciting story in the history of Israel and the one who figures most prominently in that story is an ordinary person, who, in the hands of God, became extraordinary. James said Elijah 'was a man of like passions as we are' but God took that man even with all his weaknesses and through that man He shook a nation.

The character of the prophet. One commentator says 'The most illustrious prophet Elijah was raised up in the reign of the most wicked king in Israel. We are not told anything about his parentage or background except that he came from Gilead, a wild rugged country. Its hills were covered with shaggy forests and its valleys were the haunts of wild beasts'. For one thing Elijah was a remarkable man physically. This was no city slicker. He was a man from the backwoods loving to roam over the wide open spaces or hack his way through the forests. I am sure that the rugged austere appearance of this man with bulging muscles and weather beaten skin attracted the attention of the soft-clad townsman. I think of him as shaggy bearded, long haired, suntanned, wearing a sheep skin, living in animal country, but with a bearing and demeanour that made people look at him and look again.

He was remarkable in terms of courage. Someone has called Elijah the 'Martin Luther of the Old Testament Israel', a man who single-handed challenged the whole priesthood of the state religion as well as the people in general to the test on Mount Carmel of which we read of in ch 18 and, if I may say so, challenged God. In v 36 'Let it be known today that you are God in Israel, and that I am your servant, and that I have done all these things at your word'.

He was a man of courage because he was a man of faith. What faith was required to go to Ahab, a man who was the very embodiment of evil and say to him, 'Listen your majesty, there will be neither dew nor rain these years except at my word'. We need men of faith today who will challenge the powers that be and tell them there is no hope of lasting well-being for this nation or this province until we turn from our sinful selfish ways.

He was a man of courage because he was a man of faith because he was a man of prayer. James says 'He prayed earnestly'. Elijah believed that God, not Ahab, had the last word and he acted accordingly. It's certainly clear that the life of this man was soaked in prayer and the strength he derived from that source impelled and propelled and compelled him to go to the king and deliver the message God had given him. He was able to stand before an earthly king because he practiced prostration before the heavenly King.

And all this, his courage, his faith, his prayer, because he knew the Scriptures. Elijah knew the Books of the Law e.g. Deuteronomy 11 'Take heed that your heart be not deceived and you turn aside and serve other gods and worship them and then the Lord's wrath be kindled against you and he shut up the heaven that there be no rain and that the land yield not her fruit'. Elijah took his stand on the Word of God and no man who does that is on the losing side.

He was in touch with events. He knew the score. He saw that Israel was guilty of the very sins God said He would punish with drought and famine and, as he saw the growing immorality and deepening degradation, he couldn't be quiet any longer. Who that has any understanding of the Scriptures is surprised at the depths to which this so-called Christian country has fallen , the utter breakdown in family life, the acceptance at all levels of this cursed thing called lesbianism and homosexuality, the loose sexual living of young and not so young outside of marriage and, I might add, as a matter of course, the acceptance of standards within Christian circles that would have made our Christian fathers blush with shame.

Christian, God is on our side, only as long as we are on His side. We are too like the Church at Sardis in Revelation 3. We have a name, a reputation of being alive, but we are dead. Elijah was in touch with events.

He was concerned for the glory of God and that's what matters. We are concerned about the existence of Protestantism, maybe Presbyterianism, maybe union with the United Kingdom. This man was concerned for the glory of God. That was the problem that faced Habakkuk. Habakkuk challenged God. He says 'Look Lord, why do you tolerate the unrighteous living of your own people, why do you allow your people to prosper when they so blatantly flaunt your laws?' Elijah reasons along the same lines. God has made certain pronouncements. Is He not going to carry them out? Will the people think He closes His eyes to their willfulness and sin? So he marched into the presence of king Ahab. Notice the condemnation he proclaimed.

There were things that might have deterred Elijah. Fear of the consequences. Too many of us are motivated by consequences. What will happen if we do this? Elijah took his life in his hands. Ahab was a ruthless, evil man but Elijah went into his presence. Again, what if the pronouncement came to nothing. He said "Ahab, there's going to be no dew or rain until I say so". What if that came to nothing? The prophet would be seen to be a fool and the name of Jehovah would be ridiculed. But this man was in touch with God and believed that he was in the will of God. What matter then the consequences? God honoured His servant's obedience.

Can we learn at least this. If we want to share in our own small sphere something of the success that came to Elijah, we must make the glory of God the first priority of our life and conduct. Are we doing that? By the way, Elijah had a price to pay. So may we. Jesus said 'except a corn of wheat fall into the ground and died it abideth alone, but if it die it brings forth much fruit'. Do you want your life to bear that kind of fruit for that's the kind of fruit that will last? Elijah was raised up to turn a decadent society back to God. Don't forget where that decadence began. It began with Solomon, a man highly favoured by God but because of compromise in what appeared to be a little thing, he started the nation on a slide that led to the horrible state of events outlined in the first part of I Kings.

Are you a Christian? Have you given your life to Jesus Christ? Are you really devoted to the Lord? That's what matters. May God help us to examine ourselves in the light of the situation in which we live for it is pretty awful, politically, socially, morally awful. If there ever was a time when God needed men and women to stand for Him, it's today. May God help us, never mind the consequences, to be true to Him.

APPENDIX D

SERMON SNIPPETS

It is one of the tragedies of Ulster that the message of the evangel has been brought into disrepute because of the gross inconsistencies of too many who claim to have had a born again experience.

Three things are required in this business of leadership in the Church. It must be authoritative. It must be spiritual. It must be sacrificial.

There is nothing light or frothy about a life of total surrender to Jesus Christ, and no preacher has any right to make commitment to Christ any easier than Jesus Himself did.

The Church Prayer Meeting is neglected because of the neglect of private prayer. The person who knows anything about praying at home will not be able to stay away from the place of corporate prayer.

Isn't it a strange thing that Jesus Christ was willing to humble Himself so that salvation might be brought to us; and yet we are so unwilling to humble ourselves to accept it?

If you want to be a Christian, make no mistake about this, the world will no longer want you; and if you are a Christian and you find that the people of the world are still willing to link on your arm, then I am afraid there is something wrong.

The world isn't the slightest bit impressed by the knowledge that you attend Church and help in its services, it is what you do outside that matters to them.

We cannot overestimate the importance of prayer and yet there is no act more simple.

If the Church needs anything it is warm-blooded enthusiasm.

If I am devoted to my Lord, I will live a disciplined life.

The world has nothing to offer that is comparable to authentic Christianity.

(To ministry students) You will have boundless opportunities to present Christ but the training you will receive will be of little consequence if you are without vision.

If the work of the Holy Spirit is deep and penetrating enough we see sin through the eyes of God.

Whatever stands between you and your decision for Christ is sin.

The kind of people God can use are the people who have an unshakeable confidence in Himself, and a like confidence in His Word.

The Christian who refuses to give beyond the requirements of his own church is a poor specimen of the New Testament ideal.

The enemy is steadily encroaching all because we are chocolate soldiers and not Christian soldiers.

I am more and more convinced that the one and only answer to the problems that confront communities and individuals is to be found in a deliberate decision of the heart and mind to accept God's way as it is revealed in Jesus Christ.

Christianity and social reform are closely linked, and I cannot see how a man can be a preacher of the soul-saving Gospel without condemning the soul-destroying practices that exist in our day.

Sometimes God positively engineers circumstances in order that His people may have an opportunity of witnessing for Him in the midst of trouble and bother.

If we are members of the Church and decline to give our support to the things for which the Church stands, then our interest will diminish and indeed die.

The Bible shows clearly enough that evangelism is telling about God's love for sinful man whatever the results.

FINAL WORD

Reading these pages might stimulate personal memories of John and gratitude to God for him. Perhaps you heard him preach, or speak to you individually and from his own lips you heard the gospel as he pleaded with you to receive the Saviour. What delight he would share in heaven if, because of this book, you were led to respond to that gracious invitation.

This inadequate effort to tell John's story is not intended to be in praise of John Girvan for that would be the very last thing he would have wanted. Such an idea would be anathema to him. However, it is produced in thanksgiving to God who took a very ordinary man and used him in an extraordinary way to touch the lives of many people. It is to Him alone, John's Saviour and Lord, that we would ascribe all the praise and glory.